We Are Readers

Lucy Calkins, Series Editor

Natalie Louis

Photography by Peter Cunningham

Illustrations by Marjorie Martinelli

HEINEMANN ◆ PORTSMOUTH, NH

To Mom and Dad. In our house hung a sign that read, "There are two lasting bequests we can leave our children: the first is roots; the last is wings." Thank you for these bequests in my life. I hope this book gives roots and wings to teachers' teaching, too. —Natalie

Heinemann
361 Hanover Street
Portsmouth, NH 03801–3912
www.heinemann.com

Offices and agents throughout the world

© 2015 by Lucy Calkins and Natalie Louis

The authors and publisher wish to thank those who have generously given permission to reprint borrowed material:

The Beetle Alphabet Book. Text copyright © 2004 by Jerry Pallotta. Illustrations © 2004 by David Biedrzycki. Used with permission by Charlesbridge Publishing, Inc. All rights reserved.

Three Billy Goats Gruff, by Paul Galdone. Clarion Books, Houghton Mifflin, 1973. Used by permission of Houghton Mifflin Harcourt, Inc.

Carrot Seed. Text copyright © 1945 by Ruth Krauss. Illustrations copyright © 1945 by Crockett Johnson, copyright renewed © 1973 by Crockett Johnson. Used by permission of HarperCollins Publishers.

Materials by Kaeden Books and Lee & Low Books, appearing throughout the primary Reading Units of Study series, are reproduced by generous permission of the publishers. A detailed list of credits is available in the Kindergarten online resources.

Cataloging-in-Publication data is on file with the Library of Congress.

ISBN-13: 978-0-325-07699-7

Series editorial team: Anna Gratz Cockerille, Karen Kawaguchi, Tracy Wells, Felicia O'Brien, Debra Doorack, Jean Lawler, Marielle Palombo, and Sue Paro
Production: Elizabeth Valway, David Stirling, and Abigail Heim
Cover and interior designs: Jenny Jensen Greenleaf
Photography: Peter Cunningham
Illustrations: Marjorie Martinelli
Composition: Publishers' Design and Production Services, Inc.
Manufacturing: Steve Bernier

Printed in the United States of America on acid-free paper
19 18 17 16 15   VP   1 2 3 4 5

Acknowledgments

THIS BOOK IS AN ODE to kindergarten teachers. A colleague recently asked me, "Why are you a staff developer?" Without thinking, I answered, "I love teachers!" Kindergarten teachers are in special need of care because what they do with our very beginning learners is nothing short of miraculous. Thanks for letting me join in the miracle of your classrooms.

Lucy Calkins. I almost left my thank you like that. This might be the best way to express gratitude for someone who stands for so much. But I worried that readers might not know how Lucy gave heart and soul and over a year to this project. She shouldered us and carried us on. Lucy makes every collaborator in this project feel known and needed. She believes in us and then teaches us. Lucy pushes all of us beyond what we think is possible.

Thank you too goes to Laurie Pessah, Kathleen Tolan, Mary Ehrenworth, and Amanda Hartman. Each of you brings all of who you are to your leadership positions in ways that reach out into the world and make it better.

My Teachers College Reading and Writing Project (TCRWP) colleagues are the best! Every day they show up and roll up their sleeves to give to a profession they love. I am inspired by them. I am smarter because I learn with them. All of you have my wide-eyed amazement and heartfelt thanks.

Thanks to Mary Ann Colbert. For over a decade, we have been colleagues and friends. Our conversations make me question what I believe about powerful teaching and powerful leading. Thanks for both walking by my side and leading the way.

I am appreciative of our larger literacy learning community, too! We understand beginning reading better because of Marie Clay, Irene Fountas, and Gay Su Pinnell. We learned what matters most in reading workshop and in kindergarten from Dick Allington and Anne McGill Franzen. Donald Bear and Patricia Cunningham make our word study work smarter. Joanna Uhry taught us about teaching into early reading difficulty. We teach into the potential of our earliest readers with Kathy Collins, Matt Glover, and Peter Johnston. Elizabeth Sulzby's research is the backbone of the second part of this unit. Her emergent storybook work helps us understand what comes before conventional reading.

Marjorie Martinelli's charts make the teaching in this book cleaner and clearer. Thanks to Jennifer Green of the Pegasus School in Huntington, California, for test-driving this unit with such joy. Taryn Vanderberg and Annemarie Johnson gave the draft a critical review, spotted sequence problems, and took it upon themselves to fix those problems.

Katie Clements joined this book with a combination of power and quiet grace. She read sessions and listened for clarity, and when the teaching was unclear, she gave the most perfect feedback. I felt braver, and she made revision of the book a joyful learning experience. Jean Lawler joined Katie Clements as the editor of this book, and Jean's scrupulous attention to every microscopic detail was important, as I could rest assured she missed nothing! Rebecca Rappaport Sanghvi joined Jean to help with details. Their contributions meant that my writing sail was ever tilted toward the wind.

Then there's the behind the scene team at Heinemann—and what a team. I'm grateful to Vicki Boyd, the fearless leader of the whole place, for inspiring her team to work with heart and soul. I'm grateful to *her* leadership team, including both the ever-energetic, imaginative Stephen Perepeluk and our own beloved Abby Heim, who leads all things TCRWP.

Finally, thank you to my friends and family. I want to give exploding heart thanks to Sheila Hoag. She is a second mom and cares for my children as if they were her own. Dylan and Luke grow me and bless me. And Jimmy. Thanks for taking it all over. I could cry with gratitude, but then you would just laugh. Thanks for laughing always!

—Natalie

Contents

BEND I Launching with Learn-About-the-World Books

BEND II Reading Old Favorite Storybooks

Read-Aloud and Shared Reading

An Orientation to the Unit

THIS IS YOUR CHILDREN'S first-unit-ever, marking the start of their school careers. Your biggest message is that yes, indeed, you can read! They have come to school, and now they can be readers. You will know that this unit has succeeded if, by the end of it, all of your kindergarten students declare, "We are readers!" While you will be teaching reading strategies and habits, the most important teaching you will do in this unit is about desire, identity, and belief. The ultimate goal for this unit is to create kids who *want* to learn to read and who *believe* that they can do it.

This unit is unusual in a few ways. First, most of the units in the series have three or even four parts, or bends, in the road; this one has only two. The first bend invites kids to read information texts; the second adds storybooks to the mix, so that now the kids add a new kind of reading onto what they were doing previously. That is, by the second half of the unit, reading time for your kindergartners will include time to reread and retell familiar storybooks as well as time to study the pictures and figure out words (as best they can) in concept books and other nonfiction books.

The second way that the unit is unusual relates to the first. At the start of kindergarten, you won't be able to teach a minilesson, then say, "Off you go," and expect your kindergartners to sit themselves down with a stack of books and sustain an involvement with those books for very long. However, time with books is vital to your children's growth. The answer will be, first, to devote more time to shared reading, read-aloud, and word study so that the reading workshop, for the first month or two of kindergarten, lasts for forty-five minutes rather than an hour. But the second answer is that the reading workshop itself includes five or ten minutes for one kind of reading and then similar time for another kind of reading, with each kind of reading occurring first alone and then with a partner. At the start of the unit, this translates into a time for kids to look at (to read to themselves) environmental print and information books and then a time for them to share that. Soon their reading involves also a time to read rich familiar storybooks to themselves and then to a partner.

Of course, most of your kids will be doing emergent rather than conventional reading of both information and narrative texts, which doesn't mean that their skills won't develop in leaps and bounds across the unit. They will—but the skills will include concepts of print and using knowledge of story language and structure to support emergent reading.

In the first bend of the unit, you will teach children that reading is all around them. They move from trying to read the print that is in their world to trying to read information books, and to do this in ways that allow them to learn about the world. In their learn-about-the-world books, children will learn how to read the visuals for information, and you will spend several days teaching the different purposes for rereading. The second bend has kids reading old favorite storybooks. These are books that have been read to them again and again in read-aloud. These stories are familiar enough to your kids that they can approximate reading these books during reading workshop. During this part of the unit, kids will use the pictures and their words to construct the story at first, but then will eventually—again through rereading and coaching—move closer to using some of the actual book language to "read" these old favorites.

The two bends, then, focus on nonfiction reading and rereading and on old favorite storybook reading and rereading. The two bends combine to help your youngsters develop concepts of print as well as early reading behaviors and identities.

THE INTERSECTION OF READING DEVELOPMENT AND THIS UNIT

The trickiest part about the start of kindergarten is the unknown. There's no way to know what happened before your children arrived in your classroom.

As a kindergarten teacher at the start of the year, it's a time when you feel a sense of possibility, but also a sense of anxiety. You don't know the kids—and no one else at your school does, either! It's your responsibility—but also your opportunity—to get to know the children. What an honor, really, to teach kindergarten!

Everyone wants to be known, and for your kindergartners, this is probably their first time becoming part of a larger school community. It is crucial, then, at the start of kindergarten, to make sure all your children are known. This unit includes both story and informational reading in part because this means you are able to use both kinds of reading as windows to get to know your children. As children choose which information book to read, you will discover your shark lover and your soccer fan. When kids curl up with storybooks, you will discover who lives in story. And, when some kids struggle to connect with books, you will know that finding that special book and reading it with a child in ways that make the book special to him is perhaps your most important first job at the start of the kindergarten year, at the start of this child's amazing reading life.

Your children are also four and five years old. In this first unit, in the very earliest days of kindergarten, they don't yet know how school goes. So, part of what you're trying to do is paint a picture of how things work. Children are thrust suddenly from being part of a family, or from a less formal care setting, to being part of a class of twenty-four kids in a more highly structured day. Reading workshop can be so powerful for your kindergartners because there is a way that it goes. The predictability of the reading workshop (and of the writing workshop, too) helps your youngsters learn quickly that yes, indeed, they can do this thing called school. The routine matters, the predictability matters. The crystal clear structure and the transitions between parts of the workshop all matter because so many other predictable routines have changed for your kids as they transition to kindergarten.

The name of this unit is *We Are Readers*. In a very real way, you are actually trying to show kids that they already *are* readers. As they walk through the school and read the school walls at the very beginning of the unit, their approximations are welcomed as reading. Your welcoming response to their approximations and your acceptance of their best efforts are a hallmark of this first unit. Reading has often been thought of as something that is done in one just-right way. But in this unit, you hold tight to the idea that there are a lot of ways to be a reader. Everyone is welcome, because there are so many ways to be a reader. Your kindergartners can do amazing things this year, because we

welcome all their attempts and call each of those attempts reading. Everybody joins. Nobody opts out.

In this unit, the first reading unit that most of your children will have experienced, you'll honor this approximation, first by inviting your children to read fascinating nonfiction texts—texts with flaps and mirrors and creatures with weird noses and trucks with big cranes. Then children will also read emergent storybooks—old favorites that are read over and over and over again. Both of these bends in the unit allow kids to approximate reading—they pore over the pictures and reread familiar texts, building excitement and energy all the while.

Your aim will be to draw your children toward conventional reading. You will move them toward this reading without working to fill them up with too many overt strategies—instead, for now, your efforts will go toward making sure that your children all learn that reading is something they *can* and *want* to do. When your children reach a point where they want to read a text conventionally but can't, when they are craving the skills and powers to read conventionally, then your teaching will teach them the skills they need to do that—super powers that will move them another big step closer to reading the way they by then will desperately want to read.

Actually, the truth is, while making sure that all your children develop identities and habits as readers and the motivation to read, you will also be developing the foundational skills that will allow them to take off as readers. You'll support their concepts about print (that is, their understanding that books are read from cover to cover, left to right, top to bottom), their phonemic awareness (they'll be learning to rhyme, to play with the sounds in words, to hear component sounds in a word), and their phonics (they'll be learning letter names and sounds). Some of this work will happen within this unit, and some will happen during the writing workshop, shared reading, and word study time, which parallel your reading workshop. All of this learning, however, is important to children's success during the upcoming unit.

Your kindergarten students are also people who want things to happen again and again. The constant refrain of kindergarten, "Do it again!" means that kids are primed to learn from rereading, and in this unit you lean heavily on that. Your children take comfort in and also love familiar texts. There's comfort in repetition, and indeed that's how kids learn things, reading and doing something they love again and again. In both bends of this unit, you lean into that "do it again" inclination of kids this age.

Finally, this unit also honors the language that your kindergartners bring from home. Your four- and five-year-olds may not have tons of experience with letters and sounds and words, but they do often come knowing *something* about those concepts and how they work in each of their worlds. They probably have a handful of words that they know by sight. Perhaps they already know their name as a word and the name of some other loved ones, too. They probably know some words that go with their passions, such as *soccer* or *pony* or *Pokémon*. Your kids also come to school talking. They come with their own language, their own way of saying things. This unit invites kids to bring all that they know about language to the reading of books.

OVERVIEW

Bend I: Readers Read Learn-about-the-World Books

During the first bend in this unit, the goal is to convey to children that they can read up a storm, reading by themselves and with others, and that they can learn about the world through that reading. Of course, this is week one of kindergarten, so the truth is that most of your kids can't yet decode texts on their own, which means that you'll be teaching them to approximate reading. For now, your message will be that to read, people think about what makes sense and draw on all the available information to help them figure out what the words on the page say. That is, your emphasis will be on meaning first, although throughout this bend and the one to follow, you'll also teach your kids to draw on and extend their early concepts-about-print knowledge.

The bend starts with children taking a walk through the building and "reading the school"—conjecturing that the sign above the office says "office" (even if, in fact, it says the principal's name). After the minilesson, during your first day's reading workshop time, children will also "read the room," perhaps figuring out that the sign over the block area says "blocks" and that the sign on the shelf holding books says "bookshelf."

Soon you will shift to spotlighting books (not just environmental print), and the focus will be on reading concept books, books that help children gain conceptual knowledge, such as numbers, colors, or opposites. They will also read other high-interest nonfiction books. These learn-about-the-world books should be beautiful, with flaps and pulls and features. Keep in mind they aren't the level A/B books—there's no need for that until the kids are actually reading the words. These books, instead, are probably from the unleveled section of your library. You will teach kids that they can study the pictures and try to figure out what the words say. By studying the page, they cannot only try to figure out what might be written but they can also learn a lot about their subject, about things like bug butts and fly guts and cool trucks! (Of course, if you have children who come into your kindergarten reading conventionally, those children can be steered toward the early reader books they need and also still be encouraged to peruse the nonfiction books that kids their age tend to be so excited about and enamored with.)

With such cool stuff to read, your kids will need a friend to join them during reading time. There will be a session in which you will teach your kids that work time will have two distinct parts. They will spy on you as you act out both private reading and partner reading, and you'll set them up to spend part of their time reading on their own, and then part of their time reading with a partner. It works well for partners to sit back to back during private time and hip to hip during partner time. This teaching will help with the management of your reading workshop.

There will be other minilessons, too, that help to manage the kindergarten reading workshop, but like the minilesson that introduces private and partner reading time, all your management minilessons do double duty by helping readers know wonderful things they can do as readers and also giving them productive ways to work. You'll teach your readers that when they read with partners, they can do see-saw reading (you can imagine how that goes!) or they can mark and share Wow! pages. Ways of working such as these do wonders to help focus your sometimes "unfocusable" kindergartners.

Once you show your kids how to read cover to cover by noticing the title and the title page, and once you get them to read pages from top to bottom and from left to right—you will model that after you have read a few pages—it helps to remember what you have read so far. That remembering can help a reader think about what will probably come next in the book. All of that teaching sets the stage for you to teach kids that readers reread.

Rereading is probably the most important reading behavior of them all, and so it feels just right that at the very beginning unit of your kindergarten year, you get kids rereading for different purposes. You will call kids to this work of re-seeing their books by saying, "Today I want to teach you that readers don't just whip through a book, then toss it to the side, and say, 'I'm done!' No way! Readers (like writers) have a saying: 'When you are done, you've just begun!' When readers finish a book, they think, 'Let me try that again,' and then they reread the book. *Reread* means to read again." And, with those words, you will begin several days of rereading fun!

In one session, you will try to get kids to think about putting pages together and not just tackling one page at a time. To do this you will say, "You know how each time you go back to a playground, you often discover something new? Maybe one day it's a worm poking its head in and out of the sandbox and the next day it's an old stump of a tree you've always run right past on your way to the swings." You will then turn this playground reference into your teaching point by saying that when you read a book again and again, it is just like seeing something new on the playground. You can begin to see that all of the pages go together and so are meant to be read in a *together* sort of way. Connect-the-pages words, such as *and* and *then*, will help your readers do this kind of accumulation in a text.

You will also help your youngsters to reread, trying to think more on each page. This teaching will begin with you reminding kids that they have learned so much about beetles by reading and rereading *The Beetle Alphabet Book.* You will then invite them to rethink their books by saying, "Once we know a book really well, then we have a chance to reread and add a pinch—that means just a little bit—of our own thinking, too!" You will reread a page and then reach for a Post-it with a cartoonish picture of you. Continuing, you will say, "This is me. I have to add *me* to each page!" Your kids will then practice adding "pinches" of themselves by saying, "I think—." on each page.

This bend concludes with sessions on learning from the words in books. Your kids will cheer you on as you demonstrate repeating an important word from a learn-about-the-world book, a word like *beetle*, and then searching the page to try, try, try to find that word. Your kids (and you) may feel nervous about an early emphasis on the words, but we believe that when learning to read, kids love invitations to notice the words and not just the pictures. Your kids will end this first bend with a symphony share in which, when prompted by a light baton tap, they each read a page from one of their learn-about-the-world books into the circle, using their best teacher-like voice.

Bend II: Readers Read Old Favorite Storybooks

In the second bend, you will remind children that earlier you pointed out that there are different kinds of buildings and different kinds of dogs, and there are different kinds of books, too! Some books are learn-about-the-world books, as you have dubbed concept and other nonfiction books, and others are old favorite storybooks, or the favorite fiction stories you have read aloud repeatedly. In this bend, children continue to read learn-about-the-world books to end each reading workshop, but the bulk of workshop time will now be devoted to the reading of old favorite storybooks, which you will have scaffolded with your repeated readings.

During the first part of reading workshop, then, your students will be reading these books—*The Three Billy Goats Gruff, The Carrot Seed,* and any other rich storybooks that you have read aloud half a dozen times and can get into their hands. Later, they will work with partners to scaffold the work they do independently. You can think of the reading workshop as divided into three ten-minute long strips of time: a bit for private reading of books like *The Three Billy Goats Gruff,* next a bit for partner rereading of those same books, and then, similarly, private and perhaps even partner reading of learn-about-the-world books.

Ideally, your daily schedule will include at least two balanced literacy time slots, one for reading workshop and the other for read-aloud or shared reading. As kids hear emergent storybooks over and over, their understanding of story structure and story language will grow. They will also get better at studying pictures to make meaning, and they may even begin to read some words, mostly because they will have heard and read these books so many times. This instruction, based on the research of Elizabeth Sulzby, is described in Chapter 4 of *A Guide to the Reading Workshop, Primary Grades.*

The first session in this bend begins with the giving of presents. You will wrap up the old favorite storybooks and give them to kids, inviting them to unwrap the books and to use them to fill the table tubs. Imagine the fun of kids, ripping paper from these beloved books and exclaiming over old favorites. You will declare, "These presents are the old favorite storybooks that I've read aloud to you since the first days of school." Then you will begin to teach your kids how to read these books themselves. They will not be reading these books conventionally (or even trying to do so), but still, you should refer to their approximations as reading.

You will soon need to teach your kindergartners to make sure that what they read matches the page and the part they are on in their books. You will help them understand this concept by reminding them of the singing you always do together. (It is kindergarten, after all, so of course you won't be able to resist singing with your children.) You will say, "Sometimes we get so into the song—perhaps it is the gathering song—that we stop paying attention to where we are on the page. When our singing does not match the page, we get confused and it's hard to stay together. It even gets hard to understand the words of the song!" Modeling how you sometimes get off track and then how you can back up to fix your mismatches is a powerful way to get your learners to pay attention and do the same work in their books.

Because the development of your four- and five-year olds depends so much on what happens at home, too, you will teach your kids to be their own best literacy advocates. One of your sessions will begin with a call to action that sounds like, "Today I want to teach you how to make *new* old favorite storybooks." You will teach a tiny replicable process for getting more old favorite storybooks into your collection. Your kids will find a loved one, get that person to read and reread (and reread) a book, listen closely to it, and then read it back to that loved one. This, after all, is the very process that Elizabeth Sulzby's research discovered was at work in the lives of kids who learned to read with ease.

On the one hand then, new books will be added into the table tubs. Meanwhile, kids will also get better and better at their old favorite reading. Because one of your big goals in this bend is to develop your kids' book language, you'll definitely want to teach them to add character dialogue into a story. "We really want these characters to live here with us in our workshop." Then you might reveal two stick puppets, a troll and a goat, and use these to get the kids to practice dialogue. "If we want these characters to live here, we need to make these puppets talk. They need to say the true words from the story."

As the bend progresses, you will again teach about the importance of connecting pages in books. You taught this in the first bend, but this time the teaching is in storybooks. Narrative is all about sequence, and so to help your kids find the right connecting words you will say, "You want to think about time. It is kind of like you need a *when* word, a time word as you turn the page." You then add, "Very often, your answer to this question ('When?') will help you connect the pages."

To get your kids' reading to sound closer and closer to the actual book language, you will compare their reading again to singing. You will remind them how the chorus is often the easiest part of a song to sing exactly right. It is the repeating part of the song. You will then use that comparison to teach an important reading behavior, by saying, "Did you see how in order to make my reading even better, I thought about parts of the book that repeated, and I tried to read those parts using the *exact* words from the book? Those are words I know by heart, so I can read them exactly right every time I read this book."

Before the unit ends, you will once again encourage your kids to read some of the words on the page. Because many of your kindergartners are still learning about letter and sounds and words during word study time, you will

not expect them to read the words on the pages correctly. However, your kids are probably beginning to label pictures in their own writing during writing workshop. You will show your kids that they can do this work in their old favorite storybooks, too. The title of the book, the dialogue, and the repeating parts all contain words that they can probably read a little bit.

The unit ends, like all giant endeavors should, with a final celebratory session. After getting the kids to choose and practice one special old favorite book that they will read really well to someone in the school, you could say, "In our parade today, just like the parades that teams throw when they win championships, we will want to show off our trophy to the world. *Our* trophies are books."

You will then parade through the halls of your school. Once you have warned the rest of the school and chosen a parade route, you can arrange for cheering crowds. There may be signs such as *We love kindergarten readers!* or *The Carrot Seed rocks!* After the parade and the reading, you might end by giving each child a symbolic "key to the city." You could call this the "key to the reading world in your school."

As this unit ends, you can feel certain that you have successfully launched a lifelong reading journey for your kindergarten students. You will definitely know you have succeeded when their words and actions declare, "We *are* readers!"

ASSESSMENT

Based on their early experiences with print—bedtime stories and read-alouds, big book shared reading, shared writing, and their very independent adventures with pretend reading and writing—young children come to kindergarten with different understandings about the conventions that are used to communicate meaning in print. An assessment of each child's level of understanding, and sometimes misunderstanding, of these conventions will help you know what students are attending to in print and what still needs to be learned. Chapter 6 in the *A Guide to the Reading Workshop, Primary Grades* will help you select assessments for getting to know a lot about your readers very quickly: in particular, the Concepts about Print (CAP), Letter/Sound Identification, and High-Frequency Words List.

Make careful observations about students' reading lives and habits.

From the very start, you may want to keep a class list or a conferring sheet for each child handy on your clipboard as you circulate around the classroom, observing children as they select books and talk with their peers about books. Take note of which children are already enthusiastic, avid readers and which seem lost at sea when it comes time to sit with a book. Take note of the topics your students talk about and the topics they search for in the baskets of books. Your conferring at the start of the year will probably involve assessing for concepts about print and other things, but you can also use these conversations to learn about students' reading lives in and out of school. Do they read at home? With whom? Where? Do they have a favorite book? What did they think about your read-aloud this morning? What kind of books would they like to read this year? These conversations can help you tailor the kinds of books you offer students across the day, as well as help you formulate plans for fostering strong reading lives for each one of your young readers.

Administer the Concepts about Print assessment.

The Concepts about Print assessment is a simple checklist of knowledge about books and words to help you figure out what each student knows about basic concepts, such as the difference between letters and words, and where to find the front and back of a book. You can refer to Chapter 6 in *A Guide to the Reading Workshop, Primary Grades* for details on where to find and how to administer this assessment, either formally, sitting one-on-one with each student, or by simply making observations as students read, using a CAP checklist.

Once you've gathered this information, you'll want to use what you know about your children's knowledge of basic print concepts to steer your plans for shared reading, word work, and conferring and small-group work during reading workshop. Marie Clay calls print concepts the "rules of the road" for literacy. If you see that children are still developing these basic concepts, you may want to use shared reading time to highlight book orientation, pretending to "forget" which way the book goes, putting it backwards on the easel, and then correcting the position of the book in a way that makes a fuss over the fact that books are read left to right. Then again, when you turn to a new page, you can act disoriented, "What do I read first?" and start in some totally inappropriate place, leading kids to correct you in an enthusiastic refrain. In word study, you might use student names to highlight the difference between letters and words by writing names on strips, and then cutting apart the name into letters to count how many letters are in each name.

Gather data about students' knowledge when it comes to letter/sound identification and high-frequency words.

As you come to know the kids in your class, you can expect to find a range of literacy skills and experiences. You will see some kindergartners who are still learning letter names and sounds—and you may see kids who are actually reading books in conventional ways.

After administering a letter/sound identification assessment, if a child does not know many letter names or sounds, assess that child's phonemic awareness so that you can understand strengths and needs when it comes to hearing sounds in words. Many young children are still developing an "ear" for the sounds in English. For example, *chip* and *ship* might sound exactly the same to a child who has not yet developed the phonemic awareness to discriminate between the digraphs /sh/ and /ch/. So might *cat* and *cut* when taken out of context and heard by a child with a developing sense of phonemic awareness. Playing word games, singing songs, clapping out syllables, and doing other such activities can be incorporated into literacy components across your day to support children's developing phonemic awareness.

You may also want to do an informal assessment of children's knowledge of high-frequency words by giving a child a 3″ × 5″ index card and asking him to slide it down a list of words and stop if he comes across a word he knows. Of course, the child may not know any, or he may know only a word or two. You can learn more about these assessments in Chapter 6 of *A Guide to the Reading Workshop, Primary Grades*.

Of course, you may have a handful (or more!) of children who are reading conventionally from day one. You can conduct running records to learn more about these readers. You can also find more information about running records in Chapter 6 of the guide.

Gather data on students' abilities regarding storytelling in familiar storybooks, using the Emergent Storybook Reading stages.

In the second half of this unit, your children will learn to tell a story across the pages of familiar storybooks. You may wonder, "How do I know if my children are doing this work well?" You can find the emergent storybook reading stages in the online resources that accompany this series. You can use this scale, based on the research of Elizabeth Sulzby, as one of many ongoing informal formative assessments regarding your children's progress. The scale provides examples at each stage: early emergent reading (when children might simply point to objects in the picture and name them), to using sentences and phrases and transitional words to list the events, to fluent storytelling that sounds just like the teacher (and the many steps in between).

You may decide to do a pre-assessment, using an emergent storybook, like *The Three Billy Goats Gruff*, with each student during independent reading time, asking the child to read you the story, with the book in hand. This information can help guide you in your decisions about what to teach in your minilessons, conferring, and small-group work—as well as what to highlight in other literacy components of your day. Then, at the end of the unit (during the last few days of it), you might conduct a post-assessment using the same book again or another emergent storybook, such as *Goldilocks and the Three Bears*. Of course, it would be crucial that in both instances children had heard the book read aloud a similar number of times. You can use your notes from the two assessments to track children's development as storytellers across the unit. But then again, you may not need to do this sort of formal assessment because, for now, your hands will be full helping to make sure that each child feels welcome and successful at school.

Use your assessment data to tailor your yearlong curricular plans.

At the end of this unit, you will want to take stock of your students' knowledge of concepts about print, letter-sounds, and their understanding of emergent storybooks. By the end of this unit, many kindergartners will be beginning to demonstrate an understanding of important early reading skills and behaviors, including a beginning understanding of one-to-one correspondence, pointing to words left to right. They may have some greater knowledge of letter/sounds, and will now have a strong sense of how stories tend to go, and how to tell a story across the pages. If you find that your students still need more support with this, before moving on to *Super Powers: Reading with Print Strategies and Sight Word Power* (Unit 2) you might decide to teach the unit titled "Emergent Reading: Looking Closely at Familiar Texts" from the online resources of *If . . . Then . . . Curriculum: Assessment-Based Instruction, Grades K–2*.

GETTING READY

Gather a selection of learn-about-the-world books and old favorite storybooks for students to read.

Starting in the first bend of this unit and continuing through its entirety, your children will be reading high-interest nonfiction books. You may not own a ton

of those books, in which case you'll need to make regular trips to the school and local libraries or to your school's bookroom. The good news is that you don't need to search for books that are both high interest and easy to read (something that is a bit of a challenge). You can forget about the books being easy to read and go all out for the high-interest angle. So bring on those inside-submarine books with precise drawings of all the floors within the submarine. Gather up the books with awesome photography and amazing text features. If you find books that have flaps and wheels and pulls, that's perfect. Hopefully you'll find books that teach the topics that your kids are already (or will soon be) obsessed with.

You will presumably also want to have some leveled nonfiction books on hand for children who enter your kindergarten classroom already reading conventionally. But frankly, they'll want to read the really enticing, glorious, nonfiction books and will profit from doing so. Their reading-the-words skills may be more advanced than their talking-and-thinking about text skills, so they'll still benefit from the work the rest of the class will be doing.

But here is the important thing about Bend I. While you are supporting nonfiction reading, you must also be reading aloud the old favorite storybooks that will be the mainstays of Bend II. You need to read a few of these—we suggest *The Three Billy Goats Gruff* and *The Carrot Seed*—four or five times during the first week or two of your reading workshop. And you need to make sure that you have multiple copies of the old favorite books that you read many times.

During the second bend of your unit, children will continue to read and reread the learn-about-the-world books, but now they will also be reading and rereading old favorite storybooks. The reason that you'll need the multiple copies of old favorite storybooks is so that children can do this extremely potent work successfully. There are a few challenges to this, starting with selecting those books that you turn into old favorites.

You might as well go with the two we recommend, for starters, as you'll see supports for these two books woven into the unit. But you will also need to choose other old favorite storybooks. Because your children will hear and read these books again and again, it is important that they really like them. The books should also have a strong plot with a fairly traditional narrative structure. In other words, the story should have intriguing characters, and go through a series of events and face troubles, troubles that, in the end, are resolved somehow. *Caps for Sale* works, and fairy tales work as well. *Koala Lou* works. *Harry and the Dirty Dog* works. Beware of the sing-songy list books. Stay away from books like *Brown Bear, Brown Bear* or *I Went Walking* or *Chicka Chicka Boom Boom*. Those are great books to read during shared reading, or during other units throughout the year, but they do not meet the criteria for a strong emergent storybook.

A powerful emergent storybook also has rich literary language. In other words, choose books that talk more like books do, and less like people do in more social situations. The books you'll choose to read aloud as old favorites are usually higher-level books, too. They tend to have more multisyllabic words and more sentences per page. Before finalizing your selection of books, make sure you have multiple copies (or can gather them) so that you'll be able to put a copy of each old favorite into the hands of at least half your kids the following week. Your children will reread this book a score of times, so having enough copies to put in table tubs is essential. Check the online resources for a list of recommended titles.

Select and gather books and texts for minilessons.

Gather your teaching texts for this unit, and be sure you come to know them really well. For example, Session 2 uses *The Three Billy Goats Gruff*, by Paul Galdone, and *The Beetle Alphabet Book*, by Jerry Pallotta and David Biedrzycki, to compare and contrast old favorite storybooks and learn-about-the-world-books, and to celebrate all the kinds of books the children will be reading during this unit.

Collect the necessary teaching materials.

- You will need chart paper and the teaching point Post-its for each anchor chart. (Please see the Resource Kit for the pre-made chart strategy Post-its.)

- You will also need blank Post-its to use throughout the unit so that students can flag pages.

- Decide whether you want to write the song lyrics to the "We are Gathering" song onto chart paper or print out the version in the online resources to be projected on a document camera (see Session 1 and the online resources).

- Print the "Private" and "Partner" reading signs on colored paper or card stock and either laminate or place in a plastic sheet protector so that you can use them again and again (see Session 3 and the online resources).

- Use students' names to launch a word wall so you can study one child's name each day. As you move from name to name until all of the kids' names have been studied, you can arrange their names alphabetically under the appropriate letters. Set up the word wall in an area that is accessible to students and easily seen by all. You will also want to use the class names to make a "Class Name" chart. This chart will be arranged alphabetically and will also probably have a photograph of each child.

Really, the best way to get ready to teach this first unit, the entire curriculum actually, is to surround yourself with a group of colleagues with whom you can share the journey. Your colleagues will help you teach more effectively because you can collaborate to learn from your children and improve your teaching,

READ-ALOUD AND SHARED READING

Use the read-aloud plan, in the back of this book, to help you prepare for one emergent storybook read-aloud across five days.

For this unit, *The Carrot Seed* by Ruth Krauss was selected because it is a tightly structured story and brief enough that children will be able to chime in after having it read to them a few times. They'll also be able to approximate reading the actual words. Kids love acting this story out, wagging their fingers while exclaiming, "I'm afraid it won't come up!" This model will act as a template for you to plan other emergent storybook read-alouds, using other old favorites such as *The Three Billy Goats Gruff* by Paul Galdone, *Caps for Sale* by Esphyr Slobodkina, and *Harry the Dirty Dog* by Gene Zion.

Select other types of texts you may want to read aloud.

You will also want to gather high-interest nonfiction books to read aloud, showing kids that through these books, they can learn about the world. Choose a variety of books and topics that will pique your children's interests and leave them clamoring for more. One text we use is *The Beetle Alphabet Book*, by Jerry Pallotta and David Biedrzycki, which is full of enticing pictures and interesting information about beetles.

Use the five-day plan in the back of this book to help you prepare for shared reading.

Shared reading is one of the most powerful things you can do with children each and every day. In fact, it is hard to think of anything that could be more important for your kindergarten children during these first weeks of school. Shared reading invites all your children to join in with gusto, and it helps every child develop confidence that he or she can indeed be a reader. We chose the all-time favorite, *Mrs. Wishy Washy* by Joy Cowley, for your first shared reading, because it provides an engaging storyline with expressive pictures and because the repetition in the book provides young readers an easy way to participate. The shared reading with this book (and other books) supports children's early concepts of print—book handling skills, directionality, and one-to-one matching.

The warm-up text is another favorite, the children's classic, "Jack and Jill." You will want to have lots of songs, nursery rhymes, and poems ready, so that children can read them repeatedly during shared reading. Rhyme helps young children develop phonemic awareness, which is a foundation necessary for successful reading in the future. Rhyme is also fun and creates a close community. Other favorite rhyming texts include *Willaby Wallaby Woo* by Raffi, "The Wheels on the Bus," and "If You're Happy and You Know It," just to name a few. Your charts and daily schedule can also become shared reading texts that you return to day after day.

☙ ONLINE DIGITAL RESOURCES

A variety of resources to accompany this and the other Kindergarten Units of Study for Teaching Reading are available in the Online Resources, including charts and examples of student work shown throughout *We Are Readers*, as well as links to other electronic resources. Offering daily support for your teaching, these materials will help you provide a structured learning environment that fosters independence and self-direction.

To access and download all the digital resources for the Kindergarten Units of Study for Teaching Reading:

1. Go to **www.heinemann.com** and click the link in the upper right to log in. (If you do not have an account yet, you will need to create one.)

2. **Enter the following registration code** in the box to register your product: RUOS_GrK

3. Under **My Online Resources**, click the link for the ***Kindergarten Reading Units of Study***.

4. The digital resources are available in the upper right; click a file name to download. (For any compressed ("ZIP") files, double-click the downloaded file to extract individual files to your hard drive.)

(You may keep copies of these resources on up to six of your own computers or devices. By downloading the files you acknowledge that they are for your individual or classroom use and that neither the resources nor the product code will be distributed or shared.)

Readers Read the World

IN THIS SESSION, you'll teach your kindergartners that readers read the world. A reader is someone who walks through the world on the lookout for things to read.

GETTING READY

✔ Write the "We Are Gathering" song lyrics in big letters on chart paper and hang this in a prominent spot (see Connection). 👏

✔ Reveal an anchor chart titled "We Are Readers!" during the teaching point (see Connection). 👆

✔ Take out today's strategy Post-it notes—"We can look." "We can think." "We can read."—to add to the chart (see Connection).

✔ Choose a couple places in the school building with signs that you and children can visit and "read" such as the school lobby and a bathroom (see Teaching and Active Engagement).

✔ Record the numbers 1–6, writing each number on a different piece of paper, and hang each paper next to six distinct areas in the classroom for children to "read" (see Link).

✔ Be sure that the six numbered parts of the room each contain lots of labels and other environmental print. It will be especially helpful if there are enough context clues that emergent readers can decipher the meaning of the print—for example, the label "pencils" is on the pencil can with a drawing of a pencil.

✔ Pointers or rulers for children to use to indicate what they are reading

✔ It is critically and urgently important that you refer to the Read-Aloud section at the end of this unit and do that work with *two* books in particular—*Three Billy Goats Gruff* and *The Carrot Seed*. This is in preparation for the second bend of this unit, which relies on kids knowing those books almost by heart, having participated in engaging read-alouds at least five times with each book.

MINILESSON

CONNECTION

Rally kids to the idea that they can walk through the world reading because there is so much to be read.

From my place at the head of the meeting area, I asked one table full of children, then another to join me. After I'd convened a few groups, I just gestured, "Come," to the remaining children, and as they joined the group sitting before me, I sang a "gathering song" that would soon become tradition during this transition. To the tune of *Frère Jacques*, I sang, pointing to the chart on which I'd written the words of the song:

> We are gathering,
> We are gathering,
> On the rug,
> On the rug.
> Everyone is here now,
> Finding their own space now.
> We are here.
> We are here.

After finishing a second round of the song, I said to the children, "You are gathering in a very special place. Look all around you. Do you see that you are *wrapped in books*? This is our

> ### Our Gathering Song
> ● We are gathering.
> ● We are gathering.
> ● On the rug.
> ● On the rug.
> ● Everyone is here now,
> ● finding their own space now.
> ● We are here. ☺ ☺ ☺
> ● We are here. ☺ ☺ ☺ ☺

library," and I pointed to a sign that labeled the bookshelf area, "and every day, we'll gather in this very special place for our reading workshop time.

"You can start right away, right here, right now, becoming readers."

❖ **Name the teaching point.**

"Today I want to teach you that readers walk through the world in a special way. They don't just see things. They *read* things. They read names and signs, directions and songs, too. They do this by looking at the words and thinking, 'What might that say?'" *Environmental Print photos*   *Read Signs*

I turned to a piece of chart paper labeled with the title of our first chart. As I added each bullet point, I read that point.

TEACHING

Demonstrate by taking your class to a place in the hallway containing environmental print. Recruit them to "read" a word or two, choosing words for which the meaning is well supported.

"Ready to walk and read the world?" Children nodded. I lined them up in pairs, then said, "Hold the hand of the reader standing next to you and follow me." I made a "zipped lips" sign. When we reached the school's lobby, I said, "All of you have been in this lobby and have *seen* the lobby, but I want you to know that *readers* don't just *see* the lobby. Readers *read* the lobby." I paused and looked directly at each child, to let the words hang heavy in the air for a moment.

Get these out

We Are Readers!

We can look.

We can think.

We can read.

"So if I want to be a reader in our school's lobby, I see this sign hanging over this doorway," and I pointed to the "Main Office" label on the door of the school office. "Watch me do this." I touched the sign and thought aloud, "Wait, what is that room?" and then said, "Oh, yeah!" and read "The Office."

"As a reader, am I going to say, 'Done,' and that's it for reading the lobby?" I asked, gesturing to all the other environmental print around me. "No way! I'll read here." I touched a row of pictures of former school principals, each with a name under the photograph. Pondering the pictures, I mused to myself, "Maybe these are people who work in the school? Teachers maybe? They have serious faces. Maybe they are principals?" Pointing to the letters under one photograph, I thought aloud to myself. 'Hmm, . . . What might this say?' Could it say, 'Principals'? What do you think?" One small voice said, "It probably says their names." I agreed that was what it probably said.

As you name the things that readers read, you may want to gesture to them: to the names of children in the class, to a sign that says "library," to the words of the song you've just sung.

You will want to have figured out where you'll take your kids during both the minilesson and the rest of today's workshop. You might take kids to a part of your classroom and announce, "Let's read the world right here!" You could take them to the hall right outside your classroom. If you are uncomfortable moving the class, you could display photos of environmental print, in its setting, using a Smart Board or other technology.

If, in fact, the sign says "Main Office" or "Central Office" or "Mr. Ambrose," the principal's name, you can decide if you personally feel the need to read the words. If you are uncomfortable demonstrating approximation and need to read the words, that is okay. But if a child reads, "Office," you don't want to say, "Wrong," because that reader will have done many things right. You could, however, say, "Could be. That makes sense."

ACTIVE ENGAGEMENT

Pair children and invite them to try reading in a different part of the school building to each other.

"Now it's your turn to try it. "Quiet as mice, follow me. Hold hands with the person next to you." I led the children to the bathroom. "Hey, that's where we pee!" one child said. Other kids giggled. "Normally, you're in and out of here quickly," I said. "But now, instead of just darting in and out, let's *read* it."

I pointed to the sign on the door and said, "You could start by reading this." Instead of giving them time to read it, though, I pushed open the door, pointed to the sign over the sinks and said, "And this," and then I pointed to the sign on the paper towel dispenser and added, "and anything else in here."

"This year there will be lots of times when you'll work with a friend. So, right now, if you are a girl, will you grab the hand of another girl, and you can work together to read this room. And boys, find a hand and you can go read the boy's room. Start reading!"

As they started talking, I coached, "Look closely to really see it. Use your finger." After a few minutes, kids came back out into the hallway and shared what they'd read: "Children's Bathroom," "Toilet," "Paper Towels," "Hand Dryer," "Kids Only." "Wash your hands."

Debrief in ways that help students know they can do similar work in another time and place.

Returning to the classroom, I took my seat at the front of the meeting area. "Kindergartners. You are doing what readers do." I held up my fingers to name parts of the process once more. "You now know that as readers walk through the world, they, one, look. Two, think. And last of all, three, read." Each time I touched a finger and named what to do, I also pointed to the Post-it notes on the anchor chart.

1. Look
2. think
3. read

LINK

Announce that children are readers who can walk through the world seeing, thinking, and reading.

"So from now on, know that *you* are a reader, and you can start, right this very minute, walking through the world in a special way. Because remember, readers don't just see things. They *read* things. They read names and signs and directions and songs. They do this by really seeing what is there and then thinking about what it might mean and then asking themselves, 'What might that say?'"

Invite children to read the "world" of the classroom, labeled with six numbered sections.

"You will see that I have numbered our classroom," I said as I pointed out the numbered signs in various parts of the room. "As I tap you on the shoulder and give you a number, head off to spend some time reading that part of the classroom." I tapped the shoulders of several children and told them to go to area 1, which was the block area. I did this for the rest of the class until all children were dispersed to read one portion of the room or another. "For now, read the room in a whispering voice to yourself."

Reading Environmental Print

THIS FIRST READING WORKSHOP is unique because the children are not yet reading books. Books will make their entrance tomorrow. For now, you have channeled children to read environmental print using context clues. To make this work more print-centered and to increase motivation, you might give some children pointers or rulers so they can point at whatever they are reading.

The time will be easier to manage if you don't keep kids in one area of the room for long. Every few minutes, you voice over, saying, "If you haven't yet done so, read your part of the room." "Use your whisper-voice." "Point and read!" Then a few minutes later, you can say, "There are more places to read!" and shift readers in area 1 to area 2, and those in area 2 to area 3, and so on.

As you move from group to group, be sure to see and celebrate approximations of reading. If different children read the same thing differently, don't let them fret too much. Encourage them to collect possibilities for what a word might say. In general, notice what is right about what your children are doing even if their attempts at reading are mostly wrong. Celebrate correcting behavior too.

MID-WORKSHOP TEACHING
Checking and Trying as You Read

"Readers, some of you are reading a word and then checking the first letter of the word and thinking, 'Does that look right?' Jamie, for example, read 'sink' above the sink, and then he checked the letter at the beginning: an *f*! It wasn't an *s* (/s/) for sink, so Jamie looked back again. He didn't give up! He finally got it—/f/ //f/ faucet! And I know lots of other kids are trying and trying again, too!"

TRANSITION TO PARTNER TIME
Channeling Readers to Partner with a Friend

I stood in the middle of the classroom and sang out, 'Stop, look, and listen," and then paused, and after that pause, said to the class, "Readers, whenever I do that, when I sing out 'Stop, look, and listen,' that's the signal for you to stop, look at me, and freeze. When you've done that, I'll signal and you can sing back, 'Okay' as your way to say, 'We're ready to listen.' You ready to try it again?"

Then I did it again: "Stop, look, and listen," and then after a prolonged silence, I signaled them to sing the refrain, "Okay!" I suggested they return to their reading so we could practice once more, which we did. I waited for them to be absolutely still before calling for the "Okay" refrain.

Then I said, "Readers, when you first entered this room, you noticed the things in it—the tables and chairs, books and toys. But now, you are not just *seeing* things; you are *reading* things. Kindergarten readers read by themselves, privately, *and* with others. Right now, huddle up close to a reading friend." They did this. "Now talk about how reading went today. What was the *best* part? Was anything a *big* surprise? Do you have questions that you're wondering about? Ready? Go!"

After children talked a bit, I said, "Read everything that is near you—together! Get started. Use your pointing finger!" After children read whatever was within reach, I moved them to yet another numbered area to continue reading the room together.

Turn + Talk

Finding More to Read

Ask children to think about other things they can read in the world.

At the end of the workshop, gather your kindergarten readers back at the meeting area to follow up on the learning that happened. Say, "Readers, you've already read a lot of things in our school, but the world is a big place, and I bet there are other things you can read outside of our classroom. Right now, tell the person next to you what you might read on your way home from school. In your mind, take an imaginary trip home from school, and as you pretend travel, think about places that can be read. Do you pass a sign? Are there letters on your mailbox? Turn and talk!"

I gave children a few minutes to do this, crouching down and listening in. Then I reconvened the group and shared out some of the ideas I'd heard.

"Ramon said he passes a McDonald's near his apartment. He can read the letters that spell out 'McDonald's.' Jennifer and Tonya both pass playgrounds on their way home from school, and there are signs near them. One has a dog on it and a big line through the dog. They think that sign says 'No dogs.' I have a feeling you'll all be able to read your way home!

"So, readers, remember that from now on, everywhere you go, you can read the world!"

If children arrive the next morning bursting with examples of what they read on their way home, you might want to download images containing the words and phrases they found, use them as a shared reading text, and put copies in their table tubs.

Readers Read Books to Learn about the World

IN THIS SESSION, you'll teach children that readers don't just read stories; they also read books to learn about the world.

CONNECTION

Gesture for children to gather on the rug and to join you in singing two rounds of a gathering song.

From my place at the head of the meeting area, I signaled for tables full of children to join me, singing our gathering song as they traveled. Once some of the children were in the meeting area, I pointed to the enlarged version of the song on the chart paper.

Explain that there are different kinds of books and give examples of two. Announce that the class will read both kinds of books and will begin by reading learn-about-the-world books.

After finishing a second round of the song, I said to the children, "Here we are again, wrapped in books! We have a whole world of books that we will look at during our reading workshop time." I swept my hand around the area. "And just like there are *kinds of* buildings and *kinds of* trees, there are *kinds of* books. Some books are storybooks. Storybooks tell the story of what happened to someone."

Our Gathering Song
- We are gathering.
- We are gathering.
- On the rug.
- On the rug.
- Everyone is here now,
- finding their own space now.
- We are here. ☺ ☺ ☺
- We are here. ☺ ☺ ☺

GETTING READY

✔ Display the "We Are Gathering" song lyrics written on chart paper (from the previous session) for the start of the minilesson (see Connection).

✔ Have on hand the two demonstration texts that will weave through this unit: a high-interest information book full of pictures (we use *The Beetle Alphabet Book*, by Jerry Pallotta and David Biedrzycki), which you will teach from in Bend I, and a lively story (we use *The Three Billy Goats Gruff*), which will inform Bend II's teaching (see Connection and Share).

✔ Choose a nonfiction book (a Big Book, if possible) with engaging photos to model reading about the world (see Teaching).

✔ Have ready today's strategy Post-it—"We can learn."—to add to the "We Are Readers!" chart (see Link).

✔ Fill table tubs with learn-about-the-world books for private reading time—one tub for each table of students.

✔ Display a collection of storybooks to reiterate the difference between that kind of book and information books (see Share).

✔ Introduce a Big Book information text during the share to help partners practice see-saw reading to learn information. This session highlights *The Beetle Alphabet Book*, by Jerry Pallotta and David Biedrzycki, but any other nonfiction text can be easily substituted.

✔ Make sure you are referring to the Read-Aloud section at the end of this book. Do that work with *Three Billy Goats Gruff* and *The Carrot Seed*—in preparation for the second bend of this unit, in which children will need to know these texts almost by heart.

I held up *The Three Billy Goats Gruff* and read the title, then said, "This is an old favorite storybook." I then story-told, "Once upon a time, a big, hairy, ugly troll lived under a bridge and one day . . ." I story-told for a few more sentences.

"Other books are learn-about-the-world books. These books tell all about something." I held up *The Beetle Alphabet Book* and in my best teaching voice, pretended to read that book: "There are lots of different kinds of beetles. They have antenna and wings and six legs."

"Over the next few weeks, you will learn to read *both* kinds of books. Let's start by reading learn-about-the-world books."

Remind children of the things they learned about yesterday.

"Yesterday, the reading you did helped you learn about the world. Who learned where the office is? Who learned where to put the big flat blocks? You see, you read words that helped you learn about the world."

❖ **Name the teaching point.**

"Today I want to teach you that you don't have to walk up and down the halls to read and learn about the world. You can sit anywhere, open up a book and presto! You start to learn cool things about the world."

TEACHING

Demonstrate how to read a book to learn about the world, beginning with the cover. Pose questions and correct your reading behaviors as you go.

"I'll show you how I read a book to learn about the world, and then you'll have a chance to do this, too." I opened a book to the middle and then said, "Whoops. Silly me. I forgot to read the cover first!" and I hit my head as if I didn't know what had come over me. Turning to the cover, I ran my finger around it and read 'Tractor! Pigs! Barn!' I'm already getting an idea of what I'm going to learn about: farms! Let's keep reading."

I turned to the first page and murmured to myself as I looked at it. "Hmm, . . . what will this teach me about farms?" I pointed to the picture of the tractor and said, "This is probably teaching me about equipment that farmers use." I flipped to another page and then corrected myself, saying, "Whoa! I turned the page *so fast*. I can learn more," and this time, I looked more and extracted more detail. "I'm also learning about the vegetables that farms grow." Leaning closer to the book, I added, "And about all the animals that live on farms."

Although our students will grow this year, one thing that will not change is the predictability of our reading workshop structure, which will always begin with a short ten- to twelve-minute lesson called the minilesson. *The minilesson is designed to teach students a skill that they can draw on today and any day. Session 1's minilesson didn't follow the predictable structure, which is why I discuss structure here.*

Use your voice intonation so that when you tell about storybooks, your voice is that of a storyteller, and when you tell about nonfiction books (learn-about-the-world books), your voice reflects that these are information books or books that teach us something. You can use any books and just approximate a page or two of text. You can make this point in thirty seconds.

Of course, the things you reference will be things you hope many kids read and learned from. But make this part of your minilesson speedy. Your questions will feel like call-and-response participation.

Obviously, this book needn't be about farms. Choose an interesting nonfiction book with big enough pictures that the kids can see them (or use technology to enlarge the smaller text).

ACTIVE ENGAGEMENT

Give children a chance to try this on the next page as you mentor them and then to share what they are learning with a neighbor.

"You ready to read a book to learn about the world? You ready for it to be your turn? You have good reading muscles. Show me your muscles. Okay, here goes." I turned the next page and looked at it, quietly signaling for kids to study the page. Then I said, "Turn and talk! Tell someone near you what you see and what you are learning."

Lydia and Yamilah were pointing at the picture of things growing in a field. Lydia said, "I see that this corn grows above the ground. We can see it and pick it."

"Yeah," Yamilah answered, "but sometimes things grow under the ground. Like carrots."

Behind me I heard Liam tell Joey, "I know that is a hawk in the sky. Hawks eat chickens. That hawk might come down and grab a chicken and eat it." Joey looked grossed out.

LINK

Invite children to list across their fingers the steps they just followed.

"Today and every day, readers, after our minilesson, after our time here on the rug, we are going to head off to our private reading spots to read. You have tubs full of learn-about-the-world books—that you now know how to read—on your tables. Let's look at the chart and list across our fingers what you do. One, look. You study the cover, look at all the details, then you," I tapped the second bullet on the class chart, "two, think, 'What will I learn about?' And then, three, read. You can use the picture and read the words. That way, you'll, four, learn more and *more* from your books," and I added this bullet to the chart. "Happy reading!"

You can't read this sort of teaching out of a book! The written minilesson can help you, but you'll need to lean close, look the kids in the eyes, be ready to show your muscles, and admire theirs. This is all about recruiting kids' energy. Don't, however, let the minilesson become long and talky as you ad lib.

You will now need to transition students from the meeting area to their seats for private reading time. This is the most important part of reading workshop, when students author their own reading lives—choosing their own books, talking to their buddies about cool and important parts, and reading pages that make them think more deeply.

While students are reading independently (usually, in September independent reading lasts for about ten minutes) this is your time to sweep the room with your eyes and ears. Today your work will be to help students with the expectations of independent reading so that as September evolves you can begin to confer with students individually and in groups.

ANCHOR CHART

We Are Readers!

- We can look.
- We can think.
- We can read.
- **We can learn.**

Conveying the Expectations of Private Reading Time

IN MANY WAYS, today is actually your first day of the reading workshop, because yesterday was not a usual day. So you'll want to scoot around the room, helping to induct kids into the expectations of independent reading time. If kids are distracted, you'll want to settle them down and channel them toward reading. "Rufus, where's your book? How about this one about elephants?" Tapping the cover, "What do you think about this?" Other kids will be whipping through the books. "Hey, wait a second. You are going so fast through that book. Remember how we were studying the farm book to learn more? You can do that with *your* book. Let's do that together." Then you'll want to read a page thoughtfully with the child.

Many of your students will point to items on a page and make comments. The reader of the elephant book will comment, "He is so fat!" You'll want to channel these kids toward learning about the topic by studying the book. "Yes, he is fat but what does this page teach us?" You will be teaching kids to use whatever they see on the page along with their background knowledge to learn from and to enjoy texts.

As you do this work, be sure you seize these opportunities to teach the concepts of print that are so essential. Point out to kids that they will want to read from front to

MID-WORKSHOP TEACHING   Slowing Down to Notice More

If many children seem to be whipping through books, you might stand in the middle of the room and say, "Readers, eyes up here. Can I tell you the smart thing Sammy decided? He realized he was whipping through books so, *so* fast, and he thought to himself, 'Hey, maybe I can slow down and read these books like we read the farm book.' So he reread this one page and this time, he saw so, *so* much more. That's something you can do, too. Slooooooow down and notice even *more* on each page. Try that right now."

TRANSITION TO PARTNER TIME
Sharing Observations with a Friend

I stood in the middle of the classroom and sang out, "Stop, look, and listen," and then after a brief silence, I led them in the refrain, "Okay! Great job with our signal! You're getting really good at stopping right away and looking up to listen.

"Readers, you are learning so many amazing things about the world. Aren't you *dying* to show someone what you have learned? The good news is that readers don't just read alone. They also get together with other readers and say, 'Look at what I noticed!' 'Listen to what I learned!'

"Right now, take a second to look over your books and find places that you want to share. Thumbs up if there's a page in your book that made you go, 'Oh! Wow!' or 'Whoa! No way!'" I scanned the room as children raised thumbs, some holding up their books to show off exact pages. "You can talk to a friend about these cool things!"

Then I said, "Get with someone near you and share what you noticed. Tell what you learned."

back, top to bottom, left to right. Teaching concepts about print is really about noticing and naming what readers pay attention to as they make sense of a text. So, as you are moving around in a book, you will want to add some academic terms to what you are doing. As you are finishing a page, you might say, "This little dot is a period. It tells us that this piece of teaching is over." Or, "These letters on this page are all capital letters." Remember that concepts about print are also developed across time, not just in a lesson or two.

Reading with Others to Learn Information

"We are Readers" Recruit kids to join you in reading an enlarged version of an information book, using all the bullets on the anchor chart. Channel students to take turns reading.

"Readers, we talked earlier about how there are different kinds of buildings and different kinds of trees. And you now know there are also different kinds of books. There are storybooks," and I held up *The Three Billy Goats Gruff*, "and there are learn-about-the-world, or nonfiction, books," and I held up *The Beetle Alphabet Book*. "For a while, you will be reading learn-about-the-world books and you'll learn about all sorts of stuff." I held up book covers that highlighted enticing topics.

"Let's read one together, okay? Sit up tall and make yourself look and feel very smart. I'm going to put on my professor reading glasses. You can do whatever you need to do to get yourself looking and feeling your smartest."

Two of my boys held fingers under their noses like mustaches. When I smiled, Brian answered, "Grown-up teacher men have these sometimes."

"Now, are you ready to read with someone near you? I'll show you a book (and this is a book you can *really* learn from). When I show you the book, will the person with the shorter hair start and read the cover? Then the person with the longer hair can read the next page. You can take turns. When we read in this way—taking turns with other readers—it is called see-saw reading! You ready?"

I brought out *The Beetle Alphabet Book* and tapped the cover. I said, "As you guys read this, try to learn as much as you can about the topic of beetles. You ready?"

Referencing the "We Are Readers!" chart's fourth bullet "We can learn." I said, "I know you are going to study the cover and think, 'What will I learn about?'" After a bit, I directed students toward see-saw reading with someone near them, though I was aware a lot of the kids were devoting more of their time to "Ewww, gross!" comments. My plan was to address these comments soon.

I used The Beetle Alphabet Book *just held up in front of the room for the kids to practice see-saw reading. You could use a document camera to enlarge the book and, in the end, you also can use any nonfiction book that is interesting from your collection.*

Readers Read by Themselves and with Others

IN THIS SESSION, you'll teach children the routines of private and partner reading, letting them know that during every reading workshop, they will have a chance to read privately and to read with a partner.

GETTING READY

✔ Invite a child ahead of time to be your reading partner during the teaching.

✔ Prepare to reveal a chart titled "Readers Read with a Partner" with three strategy Post-its—"Sit side by side." "Put one book in the middle." "See-saw read." (see Teaching). 👆

✔ Choose a nonfiction book about a topic children will like, one with engaging, close-up pictures (see Teaching).

✔ Be sure the table tubs are brimming with engaging information books for kids to choose from (see Active Engagement).

✔ Prepare a double-sided sign with a picture of a child reading alone and the words "Private Reading" on one side and a picture of partner reading with the words "Partner Reading" on the other side. This will be your signal to children throughout the unit to indicate whether they will be reading independently or in partners (see Active Engagement). 👆

✔ Establish partnerships and share the information with children prior to reading workshop (see Active Engagement and Transition to Partner Time).

✔ Add some Post-it notes to the table tubs (see Mid-Workshop Teaching).

✔ Make sure you are referring to the Read-Aloud sections at the end of this book. Do that work with *Three Billy Goats Gruff* and *The Carrot Seed* in preparation for the second bend of this unit, in which children will need to know these texts almost by heart.

MINILESSON

CONNECTION

Direct students to bring a learn-about-the-world book from their table tubs to the rug and to sit next to their assigned reading partner.

"Readers, before you take your spot on the rug next to your reading partner, please choose a learn-about-the-world book from your table tub. Bring it with you and place it in front of you. You will be using this during today's lesson." I allowed a few extra seconds for children to follow these instructions.

Help students recall how much fun it was to read at their tables and how much fun it was to read together on the rug during the share.

"Yesterday, I told you that there are different kinds of books. We will read two kinds of books during this unit: learn-about-the-world books and old favorite storybooks.

"But guess what? There are not just different kinds of *books*. There are also different kinds of *reading*!

"Thumbs up if you love reading on your own, privately, at your table!" Lots of thumbs went up.

"Thumbs up if you love reading together with a friend on the rug!" Again, there was an enthusiastic show of thumbs.

"I'm glad this room is filled with readers who love *both* reading privately and reading with friends."

❧ Name the teaching point.

"Today I want to teach you something that every reader in the whole wide world knows. Every reader, from here to China, knows that it is fun to read all by yourself, privately and quietly. And it is *also* fun to read with a friend."

TEACHING

Invite children to spy on you as you demonstrate private reading, noticing the fun things you do while reading alone.

"Let me try both kinds of reading, and will you spy on me, whispering to each other about what you see, ever so quietly? See if you get ideas for the fun things that readers do. Remember that spies are super-duper quiet, so if you see me do something fun, don't go 'Oh, oh, look!' Instead just signal to your fellow spy, someone near you, and *whisper* if you need more than hand signals."

I got myself a juicy nonfiction book, one with cool close-ups and gadgety pages and started reading it to myself quietly, making faces and noises to match my reactions. On pages where there was gross stuff, I groaned. On pages with lots of information, I acted as if I were putting more and more facts into my mind and remembering them. I tapped my head as I listed all the things I was learning and muttered to myself, saying things like, "Oh, now I get it!" and "Wow, I never knew that!" All of this took about ninety seconds.

"Spies, did you learn any fun things that readers do when we read to ourselves?" I asked and then channeled the kids to compare notes. "Tell each other," I said.

As the kids talked, I listened in. They said things like, "You were having feelings about the book." "You were talking to yourself." "We saw you tapping your head!"

"Good spying! You are right that I do all those things when I read by myself."

Demonstrate reading with a partner—a child in the class—so that children can also spy on your partner reading.

"Are you ready now to spy as I do something different? I'm going to read with a partner! Watch me."

I then shifted and for sixty seconds read with a child who was prepared to be my partner. I put the book between us so that we could both see it well, and I encouraged my partner to read the book in unison with me and to enjoy it in ways that showed the fun of reading with a friend. I made sure to look at and to talk to my partner as we made sense of the pages together.

Again, my spies whispered to share what they were learning. Then I solicited their observations: "You asked Lydia a question and then you turned pages to try to figure it out." "You put the book in the middle and you both took turns."

Today is an exciting day because formal partnerships are established! Although you are still getting to know your students, it will be important to play matchmaker today and pair students up as best you can. If you know that two students are buddies from preschool, then you have a match! If you know that two students have dogs, then you have a match! Don't fret too much about these partnerships, because once you have completed your reading assessments, you will be changing them up before entering Unit 2.

It might be helpful to take pictures of these two new partners reading and talking about books. On a pocket chart, display their pictures alongside their names written on sentence strips for a reminder. The reading opportunities with this chart alone are endless!

At the start of the year, students typically work with a partner for an additional ten to fifteen minutes after private reading time.

Any book with engaging pictures will work well for this lesson. While we sometimes indicate books that we feel work nicely, there is no need to use any one specific text.

Debrief. Name what you have done that you hope readers will do every time they read with partners.

"Good," I said and added, "That's just what my partner Lydia and I did! *First*, we sat elbow-to-elbow, knee-to-knee, like this." I pointed to my partner sitting beside me. "*Then*, we put the book right between us, like this. *Next*, we took turns see-saw reading like we learned to do yesterday. That was so much fun!"

I brought out a new anchor chart—"Readers Read with a Partner." "Readers, here is a new chart to help us remember all the fun things we can do during partner reading time!" I added the strategy Post-its to the chart, reading each one as I placed them.

ACTIVE ENGAGEMENT

Invite children to try a teeny bit of reading privately, doing this with their own nonfiction books.

"You ready to try it yourself now? It's so fun! You each have a learn-about-the-world book with you. I thought we might practice right here on the rug before we go to our tables to start our private and partner reading time. Let's pretend to do a teeny-tiny miniature reading time (doing a whole reading time in just a teeny tiny three minutes) so you can see what it is like to do some private reading and then switch and do some partner reading. We're going to have to do things super fast."

The kids looked a little lost but I pressed on, knowing it would soon make sense.

"You ready to do some private reading, only super fast, just for two minutes? You can read, and laugh, and point to good parts. You ready? Let's pretend like you just took a book out of your table tub." I held up a double-sided sign that featured, on the one side I showed, a single child reading a book, with the word "Private." I said, "This sign will be your signal to read privately, to read alone. Let's do it!"

Moving quickly, I looked down at my book, hoping the kids would do the same. I flipped through some pages, looking intently. I mimed "Wow," to make a note of my thinking.

Direct students to switch from private to partner reading, using the prepared sign to indicate the switch. Make this a quick try.

Then I paused. "Readers, eyes up for a second. Watch this." I turned the sign over so that now it said "Partner," and showed two kids reading one book together. Malachi called out, "And that says 'Partner' because those kids are reading together."

I gave him a thumbs up, read the words *Partner Reading*, and then said, "Sit up tall so I know you're ready to give partner reading a try!"

Once the kids' backs were all straightened, I signaled for them to begin to read with partners, one book open between the two of them. The kids scooched closer together (with a good bit of my scooching help), placed a book across their collective laps, and dove in.

I moved around quickly to coach into their see-saw reading. Mostly, my students needed help with turn taking.

LINK

Express how lucky the class is *not* to have to read in such teeny tiny time blocks each day, and share that from now on they will have time to read both on their own and with a partner.

"Readers. Eyes up here, please. You just did a *whole* reading time in just a few minutes!"

"It was awesome!" Liam said.

"It *was* awesome," I echoed. "But you know, it also got me thinking how thankful I am that we have more than just a few minutes each day for reading workshop! Watching you just now, I felt so happy knowing that we get to spend big chunks of time each day," and I spread my arms wide, "reading! Thank goodness reading workshop is not over so fast every day now."

"You know now that readers all over the world have two important parts to their reading lives. You can have those parts to your reading lives from now on, too! Every day you will have time to read alone, during private reading time, *and* you'll have time to read together during partner reading time. Both are so much fun.

"As you read today, keep in mind the kinds of fun things you can do when you read privately and when you read with a partner." I turned the sign over so that it read "Private Reading" and directed kids to their private reading spots, reminding them to take their learn-about-the-world books back to their seats with them.

When your students switch to partner reading time, you will want to think about where they will sit. Because your kids are reading out of book tubs (and not more portable book bags or boxes, as they will be eventually), they will probably need to sit at tables. A simple way to help kids make a smooth private-to-partner time transition is to assign partnerships a table spot (which might not be their regular table spots). Then during private reading you can teach them to turn their chairs back to back. When it is partner time teach your kids to turn their chairs back toward the tables so they can sit side by side.

Being a Proficient Partner to Launch and Lift Children's Partner Reading Work

THE BIG NEW WORK FOR TODAY is the addition of partner reading time. This can be an incredibly important time for your kids, but for that to happen, you need to invest yourself in making the time work.

As you flip your sign to signal that it is time for kids to read together during partner reading, be ready to help all your kids sit knee-to-knee with a partner, putting the book in the middle. More than that, help them know they can read by taking turns (although there are other options that you will introduce soon). Once the logistics of partner reading time are underway, you'll want to show readers the ways that partners can support each other so that reading together lifts the level of their work together.

MID-WORKSHOP TEACHING
Getting Ready to Read with a Partner

"Readers, in a few minutes, you will have time to read with a partner, so I wanted to tell you that when I am about to read with one of my reading friends, I get ready to share. This is how I do that. I save up things to show my reading partner. Sometimes I use Post-its to mark those pages I want to share, or sometimes I just list across my fingers all the things that I have read about that I want to tell my partner." I demonstrated this briefly with one of our learn-about-the-world books.

"Right now, will you read your books and get ready to share them with your partner? Remember, you can think about things you want to tell your partner and list them on your fingers or mark them with a Post-it note that you'll find in your table tub. Try that right now!"

As kids continued to read, I said, "Oh! I love it! I see some of you counting across your fingers all the things you have learned from a book. You are *definitely* getting ready to share!"

TRANSITION TO PARTNER TIME
Preparing Children to Work with Partners

"Readers, eyes here, please. As you get ready to spend time with your partner, I just want you to remember that your job is to do this reading work *together*. It's not always easy to work with a partner, but I promise that if you try your best, it is always worth it. It is so much fun to read with friends."

To give this moment a bit of formality, I added, "Let me see you signal your willingness to try hard at being partners from now on. Please join pinkies with your partner and say, 'I promise, partner.'" The room filled with pinky swears and I got ready to listen closely as partners shared.

A proficient partner conference can be an effective way to improve their work together in this session. To begin ask one partnership if you can join them as a third partner. Then as you and the others take turns reading, watch for instances when a reader flips past a page before actually studying it. "Wait, wait, you skipped something," you can say. "Let's go back and really study what is on the page." If a reader just names one thing on a page, you can say, "Wait! Let's see and say more."

When scaffolding readers to do more than they might do without you, it is always important to be aware that your support needs to be temporary and to plan a way to withdraw those supports. So you need to plan how you will exit from your temporary role as third partner. As the partners begin to work better, you might physically move from your spot between the two partners to a spot off to the side. Fewer words are always a way to decrease scaffolding. Less physical presence can be, as well!

Of course you may decide to confer into private reading time as well. Upcoming sessions will help you do that.

Celebrating Positive Partner Reading Qualities

Invite children to recognize their positive reading behaviors by sharing what you observed.

As the class gathered back on the rug, I said, "I watched you all reading today. You were reading both privately and with a partner, having so much fun. It was amazing to see."

I looked at each of them and smiled. "I wished you could have been watching what I was watching. So I thought the next best thing would be for me to just share what I saw so that we can celebrate it together. Let's try that. When I name something amazing, would you shake your hands in the air in silent applause?" I did this to show them what I meant.

"Ready? I saw some of you leaning in close to your partners to really listen to what they were saying." As I said this, I leaned my body, pretending to really listen. I then gestured for kids to do their part, and they shook their hands in the air.

"I saw kids turning to just the right page to try to answer a partner's question." This time, I just looked up and soon kids' hands were shaking wildly.

I called out the last two observations quickly, and after each one, kids gave me silent applause.

"Some kids were reminding their partner to take turns.

"And other kids were slowing their partner down so that they could really look at the pages more carefully."

After listing a small handful of positive partner behaviors, I said, "You see how much there was to celebrate in our workshop during partner time? I'm so happy that from now on, we get to do partner reading every day!"

Be sure to notice the teaching embedded in this share. Positive partner reading qualities are worth noticing and naming for your kindergarten students. Often, little kids do great things by accident. Teachers can name those great things so that kids know they are worth replicating.

Even though we suggest some qualities to name, be on the lookout for other happy accidents that are worth teaching to all of your partnerships.

FIG. 3–1 Private reading is often done with two children back to back.

Readers Read a Book from Cover to Cover

IN THIS SESSION, you'll teach children that readers read a book from the cover to the pages to the end—or from the front cover to the back cover.

GETTING READY

✔ We suggest you precede this lesson with a shared reading (such as is modeled in the section at the end of this unit), and specifically we suggest the story-book *Mrs. Wishy-Washy*, by Joy Cowley. The book either needs to be enlarged on a Smart Board or document camera, or you need to use a Big Book.

✔ Pointers or rulers to use to indicate what you are reading (see Connection)

✔ Choose a demonstration text where the picture on the cover provides a clue about the title. We suggest *The Beetle Alphabet Book*, by Jerry Pallotta and David Biedrzycki (see Teaching).

✔ Choose a second text with a picture on the cover that indicates the title (we use *Trucks*, by Wil Mara) (see Active Engagement).

✔ Display the Private Reading and Partner Reading sign (see Link and Active Engagement).

✔ Place the "Readers Read with a Partner" chart on the easel and prepare today's strategy Post-it—"Share Wow! Pages"—to add to the chart (see Transition to Partner Time).

✔ Be prepared to begin assessing kindergarten literacy skills (see Conferring and Small-Group Work).

✔ Be on the lookout for a partnership that works well together (see Share).

✔ Make sure you are referring to the Read-Aloud section at the end of this book. Do that work with *Three Billy Goats Gruff* and *The Carrot Seed* in preparation for the second bend of this unit, in which children will need to know these texts almost by heart.

MINILESSON

CONNECTION

Remind children that even though it is Day Four of kindergarten, they are already readers who can read the world and learn about that world by reading nonfiction books.

As we finished a shared reading of *Mrs. Wishy-Washy*, I stood up to point to our schedule of the day chart. "In just our first days of school, you have already done so much reading! You have been reading learn-about-the-world books *and* you have been reading the world around you. Liam noticed that on our classroom door it says 'Class K-103.' Sophie told me that she noticed it says 'Dairy' above the milk at the supermarket."

Pointing to the words *Reading Workshop* on our schedule of the day chart, I said, "And right now, we are ready to start this part of our day. Can you read what this says?" I circled my pointer around the picture of kids holding books. I pointed to each word—*Reading Workshop*—and nodded my head toward my kids to invite them to chime in with their reading voices. Lots of children called out, "Reading workshop!"

Sitting down, I said, "See. I knew it! You are already readers. Because you are already reading, I need to make sure that I am teaching you my very best tricks for reading books—the tricks that will help you really understand your books. Thumbs up if you're ready for the first trick!" Kids so signaled, and I proceeded.

❖ **Name the teaching point.**

"Today I want to teach you that when readers read books, they read the cover first, then they read the first page, the next, and the next—all the way to the end."

TEACHING

Demonstrate how you study the cover of a learn-about-the-world book and use the picture try to figure out the title.

"Who remembers, earlier today during shared reading, when we were reading the storybook *Mrs. Wishy-Washy*, the way we studied the cover and figured out the title?" The kids all signaled that they remembered doing that. "You do the same work when reading a learn-about-the-world book, too!

"Let me show you how that goes in this book." I held up *The Beetle Alphabet Book* and I thought aloud. "I see a bunch of bugs. Right here, I see a ladybug." Luke called out, "There is another one too!" I continued with a smile. "Do you think that might be what these letters say?" I asked and pointed to the title, *The Beetle Alphabet Book*, and misread it as a kindergartner might, saying, "The Bug Book.

"Who thinks that is the title of this book? You do? 'Cause the cover has a bunch of bugs on it, so that makes sense?" I spoke as if this title was an entirely logical suggestion, as indeed it was. "I wonder if each page will show a different one of these bugs and teach us a little bit about each one."

Show children how you move from reading the cover to reading the title page and first pages, revising your thinking as you go.

Opening the book to the title page (recall that it actually says, "The Beetle Alphabet Book"), I paused, pointing to the pictures of four ladybugs. "Hmm, . . . These are just ladybugs," I mused. Returning to the cover, I said, "Even though the title page has just ladybugs, I still think this is a book about a lot of different bugs because of the cover. I still think the title for the book is *The Bug Book*."

Continue reading to the last page to show how important it is to finish reading your nonfiction book.

As I turned past the middle pages, I said, "I want to make sure that I am putting together *all* the pages when I read—especially the last page, the ending." I held up the last two pages. "Look how this book ends. This page has a big *Z* and little *z* here in the corner. Now I am thinking that this book might be a letter book with all of the letters."

Turning to the very last page, I said, "This page has a bunch of little bugs on a tree." I leaned in closer to really look at the picture and then added, "There is some writing on this tree."

ACTIVE ENGAGEMENT

Challenge children to try a tiny bit of the work at the beginning of another book.

"Now it is your turn. When I say, 'Go,' I want you to sit like partners, book in the middle and knee-to-knee to begin the work of reading this book." I held up *Trucks*, by Wil Mara. "Don't forget to study the cover. Use that to think about what the title might be, and then imagine what the inside pages are about. What are they teaching? Ready? Go."

*Even though most of your kids will probably not be actually reading the title of this book, you may be wondering what to do if a child **can** read the title. You don't want to say that their reading is wrong, especially if it is not, just because they are doing the unusual. This would confuse your new reader. You probably also do not want to cheer the current reading too much or else you risk discouraging other reading approximations. You might just give a nonverbal signal to the right reader—such as a slight head nod—to let them know they got it.*

Any book with a picture on the cover that indicates the title will work well for this lesson.

Children will probably just guess at the title, forgetting to use that beginning work to help them imagine how the book will go. Be ready to push partner after partner to think based on the title.

I moved quickly around the rug, listening in as children talked. I nudged students to consider what the book might teach, not only what the title might say. Students shared, "I think it says, 'Truck' because that's a big truck." "It's going to teach you about trucks." "Maybe inside it will have a lot of trucks. Maybe there's going to be a dump truck and a garbage truck."

Moving back to the easel and turning to the next page, I said, "Try using what you figured out from the title to help you read this page." I listened in as kids talked about the new page exclusively, not carrying over the content from the title as I'd suggested.

"Readers, remember to remember! Remember to remember what you have read already," I said. "On this page, you could have done that by saying something like . . .

"Let's try one more page together," I said. I turned the page, and we did this.

LINK

Send children off to read their books by building from the beginning, page by page, to the end.

"Today as you head off to the tubs of learn-about-the-world books on your tables, remember to first read the cover, then read the first page, and the next, and the next, all the way to the end. Put *all* the pages together so that you really *understand* your books.

"Remember that you will have time to read by yourself and then time to read and talk with your partner."

Reaching down, I picked up our sign and displayed the side that said "Private." "Tables one and two," and I pointed silently to the words on the sign. After a brief pause, Malachi said, "Private!" I gave him a quiet thumbs up and I sent everyone else back to their tables to read.

Supporting Management and Assessing Concepts of Print

TODAY you'll be apt to divide your time between helping to keep kids on course and doing some initial assessments. Like the performer at the circus who needs to keep twenty plates spinning at one time, you'll need to run between your readers, using a light touch to keep up their momentum, especially for those readers who begin to falter. If you have made little Post-it note representations of the strategies you've taught so far, you can leave any one of those notes as a special reminder to a given child. "I can see you're stuck. This is a special reminder of something you can do whenever you read your learn-about-the-world books," you can say. With one child you might leave a Post-it showing a magnifying glass and a picture of a book under it ("Look closely! See more!"). With another child you might leave another reminder note, again capturing teaching you have already done. You could also leave tips with partners. You might use visuals to stand for strong partnerships qualities (as in the Session 3 Share). Later, you'll suggest to children that all these tips can get collected on a class chart that is visible to all, but for now, personalizing your tips will pay off.

As you keep kids engaged and productive, you'll want to teach them to be self-sustaining, independent learners. You'll find yourself barraged with opportunities to teach independence. When a child comes to you and whines, "I'm finished," resist the temptation to channel another book her way, and instead, nudge the child to problem solve on her own. "So why are you here?" She'll say that she doesn't know what to do next—and presto! "Hmm, . . . What *could* you do, do you think?" you can ask. After the child generates a suggestion ("Read another?"), you will want to make the point that actually, she didn't need to come to you at all. "You can solve your own problems!" you can encourage.

You can also support independence by inculcating in kids a sense of the rituals and structures of the classroom. This requires a special consciousness. Whenever you ask the kids to do anything that requires management, make sure you word your request so that you are teaching them not only what to do at this moment, but also, that you are helping socialize them to know how readers behave most of the time. So if you want kids to be better at listening to each other, you might say, "Whenever you share with a partner, always remember that partners listen with their *whole* body. Make sure your body is huddled up close, your eyes are looking at your partner, and your ears are listening carefully."

You will also want to spend some time today conducting some early assessments, and you'll want to do so while you move around the room. You might use a whole-class data sheet like the one shown here to help you record what you are noticing. The good thing about these data sheets is that they keep you from sitting in a corner, assessing one child at a time. Frankly, for your reading workshop to succeed, you need to be present in it. You'll find you can carry this on-the-go concepts about print assessment with you, making notes while still interacting with the kids. If you sit at any table of readers, you can quickly note which of them holds and moves through the book correctly. You can take just a minute or two to ask kids to point to letters or to lines of text, as the assessment asks. You will want to collect a little information about a lot

(continues)

MID-WORKSHOP TEACHING
Readers Mark Pages That Surprise Them

I stood in the middle of the classroom and called the students' attention. "Readers, in a minute, you'll have some time to read with a friend. I bet there are parts of your book that you want to read and talk about together. In learning-about-the-world books, there are often pages that surprise us. Thumbs up if there's a page in your book that made you go, 'Oh! Wow!' or 'Whoa! No way!'" I scanned the room as children raised thumbs, some holding up their books to show off exact pages. "You can use a Post-it note to mark those Wow! pages so that you can talk about them a bit later, when you have partner time. Try that now!"

of kids, moving quickly among them, rather than hoping to be comprehensive in your assessments of a few. Do not worry—you have tomorrow.

Along with assessing students during the reading workshop, you might consider setting aside some time each morning and during the day to continue assessing students' literacy skills. Some of the assessments might include:

- Concepts about print
- Letter-sound identification

- High-frequency word reading
- Phonological awareness
- Spelling
- On-demand writing

The information analyzed from these assessments will transform your teaching. You will now be armed with information that will enable you to make instructional decisions. You will be able to use data to plan for teaching that meets the needs of every student.

TRANSITION TO PARTNER TIME
Inviting Children to Share Pages with Their Partner.

I flipped the class "Private Reading" sign over to signal that partner reading was in session. "It's time for . . ." I trailed off to invite the children to read the sign aloud. "Partner reading!" voices filled in. "Yes, that's right! Make sure to sit side by side, take turns, and put one book at a time in the middle, between the two of you. Read and talk about one book together, then the next, the next.

"And remember, one thing you can do today is talk about the parts that were surprising in your books. If you put Post-its on the pages that surprise you, you can open right up to those pages! Then you can study the page that wowed you together and talk about what the page means. That's great work for partners to do together." I added a new strategy Post-it to the partnership chart:

ANCHOR CHART

Readers Read with a Partner

- Sit side by side.
- Put one book in the middle.
- See-saw read.
- **Share Wow! pages.**

Share Wow! Pages.

Name	Book Handling	Pictures vs. Print	Left to Right/Top to Bottom	Page Sequencing	Letter vs. Word	Return Sweep	1:1 Match	Punctuation	Letter Name ID	Letter Sound	High Frequency Words

FIG. 4–1   A Concepts About Print assessment

Observing the Moves of an Effective Partnership

Fishbowl a partnership who worked especially well together.

I set one partnership up in the middle of a fishbowl, formed by a surrounding circle of the rest of the students, and instructed the "fish" to do exactly what they had done during partner time, reenacting their talk.

I turned to the circle of observing students and told them, "You have an important job to do. You are going to watch two kids doing partner time. Will you help me to watch them really closely so we can notice all the things they do to make their partner time super strong? Are you ready to notice *everything* you can? When you spot a super strong partner move, put a finger up. Let's see how many moves you can count." I signaled for the partnership in the fishbowl to begin.

As the partners talked, I voiced over quietly to the observers. "Hmm, . . . notice where they put the book—between them!" I put one finger up, as if counting one strong partner move. "And look at the way they're sitting next to each other," I held up a second finger. As the partners opened up to a page with a Post-it note, I voiced over again, "Hmm, . . . did any of you notice another move just now?" Children held up three fingers, signaling that yes, they too had seen another move.

After another minute, I stopped the class and prompted them to turn and talk, naming out all the moves they had noticed the partners make.

Pulling the class back together, I said, "Boys and girls, *all* those super strong moves you noticed Eva and Michael make are the same things you can do during partner time. That way, you can help make your reading work even stronger. Thumbs up if you plan on copying some of Eva and Michael's strong moves tomorrow! Awesome!"

Fishbowl is a great method to help kids get a clear image of the work you want them to do. Fishbowl works especially well with kindergartners because they are always calling, "Hey, Watch me! Watch this!" Their desire to be admired serves as extra motivation for them to work in fishbowl-worthy ways. Video is an alternative: You can film your partnerships working together and then play back their work for everyone to study and learn from in an inquiry lesson. After all, everyone wants their 15 minutes of fame!

Readers Reread

IN THIS SESSION, you'll teach your kindergartners that readers reread and monitor themselves. Prompting readers to monitor for meaning (checking if they missed any information) early on will definitely benefit them when they begin to pay attention to print too.

GETTING READY

✔ Choose a demonstration text, either a Big Book or a text you can put under the document camera. This text should have a balance of engaging pictures and matching words. We suggest *The Beetle Alphabet Book*, by Jerry Pallotta and David Biedrzycki (we also used this text in Session 4), but lots of other books would work (see Teaching, Active Engagement, and Share).

✔ Take out today's strategy Post-it—"Reread to learn more."—to add to the partnership chart and be ready to add today's strategy Post-it—"Reread to learn more." (see Active Engagement).

✔ Concepts about Print assessment sheet (see Conferring and Small-Group Work)

✔ Private Reading/Partner Reading sign (see Transition to Partner Time)

✔ Make sure you are referring to the Read-Aloud sections at the end of this book. Do that work with *Three Billy Goats Gruff* and *The Carrot Seed* in preparation for the second bend of this unit, in which children will need to know these texts almost by heart.

MINILESSON

CONNECTION

Remind readers how they read all the parts of their books yesterday from cover to cover.

"Yesterday, after the minilesson, I watched you walk back to your reading spots, and *so* carefully, you started with the cover and the title of your book. But the really cool thing was that when you turned to the pages, you used what you read on the cover—the title—to help you make sense of what came in the early pages of the book! And then, you kept doing that. As you moved from page to page all the way to the end, you worked hard to use what you had already read to help you read more." I looked out at the children and said, "How many of you remember doing that?"

Many children signaled that they'd done that and Lola said, "I did that reading in my flower book. Flowers and butterflies." Patrick answered, "Yeah! I read like that in my counting book!"

Smiling, I continued, "Today, though, some of you told me that you would need new books because you already read the ones at your table. I was a little surprised at this. I thought, 'There's no way they've seen *everything* inside these books with only *one* day to read them!' I was thinking that *one* day with a book could never be enough. That's when I realized that we might have some different ideas about reading books."

❖ Name the teaching point.

"Today I want to teach you that readers don't just whip through a book, then toss it to the side and say, 'I'm done!' No way! Readers (like writers) have a saying: 'When you are done, you've just begun!' When readers finish a book, they think, 'Let me try that again,' and then they reread the book. *Reread* means to read again."

TEACHING

Demonstrate for children two different kinds of reading: fast, one-time-through reading and rereading.

I held up *The Beetle Alphabet Book* for children to see and said, "Remember this book from yesterday? Well, I *could* be the kind of reader who reads like this." I read, by making up words to match the picture, the last two pages aloud, snapped the book shut, and tossed it back in the bin. Then I grabbed a new book.

"I *could* be that kind of reader who whips through this whole bin of books, reading one book after another, after another, after another." I said, breathlessly. "But what I know is that books, especially learn-about-the-world books, are meant to be reread. Remember that *reread* means to read again. There is so much I can see on just one page if I take the time to *re*read it.

"So even though I *could* read my books like that, whipping through them, let me show you how I *should* try to read my books—so that I can see and learn so much more."

This time I read the last two pages of my book and then closed it, keeping the book on my lap. After a brief glance at the other books in the bin, I turned my book over and began to reread it.

Demonstrate what it looks like when you reread a page, saying what you learned the first time, and trying to see new information you missed on your first read.

"You saw that, right? I am now back to the beginning of our *Beetle Book*. Watch me now as I reread this page, about the black back beetle."

I thought out loud. "I remember reading about the black back beetle's long antennae. They look longer than his legs. And I also remember reading his big red eye. Hmm, . . . what did I *not* read before?" I made a point of slowing down to study the page, then said, "Oh! Here's something new. I didn't notice before the little bug inside the letter *b*. I think this is maybe the shape of the black back beetle. And I didn't see this green stuff coming from his," and I lowered my voice to say, "butt."

After pausing for some butt giggling from kindergartners, I added, "Maybe this is like a poison. Like a way he keeps other bugs away. Like a bug fart."

Debrief. Point out that you would have missed information if you hadn't reread.

Addressing the class, I said, "Did you notice how I *reread* the page? At first, I just noticed the same stuff I read the first time. But then I *slowed* down to try to see more. When I did that, I was able to see some new stuff on this page—the little bug shape and the green poison. I might have missed those two cool things if I hadn't reread this page!"

It can be tricky to see more in pictures as an adult. Sometimes, because we can read the words, we do not look closely enough at the pictures, noticing and naming all the little things. It can help to drag your finger slowly across all the parts of the page, putting words to what you touch. Close picture reading can take practice, but your modeling really matters. In some ways, learning to pay attention is the most important kindergarten skill of all. Your quality picture reading sets the stage for quality picture reading by your kids.

ACTIVE ENGAGEMENT

Set up children's rereading practice by reading a page in your book.

"Let's practice together now. I am going to read you this page." I read it by using the pictures only. "These beetles are fighting each other and they have short antennae."

Invite your kindergartners to reread the page you just read, slowing down to see more.

"It's your turn now. When I say, 'Go,' I want you all to take over for me. I want you to reread this page with a partner. Remember that rereading involves seeing again. Make sure you slow down and push yourself to see more so that you can learn more. Ready? Go!" I added the new Post-it to the anchor chart.

I moved around the rug and listened in as kids reread the fighting beetle page. I could hear them saying mostly all of the same things I had already read to them. I called above their talk, "Readers, don't forget to slow down and see more. Try to do that, if you haven't already. Look for something new on this page—something we missed the first time.

"Like, I heard Malachi and Aiden telling each other that these beetles have antlers kind of like reindeer do. That was something we didn't read the first time we read this page. Now, you try to find something new too!"

LINK

Congratulate children for trying to see something new on a familiar page, and remind them what this rereading work will look like in the reading workshop.

"Bravo, kindergartners! Most of you got to the part of rereading when you discover something new. Even though we already read this page, you were able to learn even more because you went back to it, slowed down, and pushed yourself to see more! Rereading does that for you.

"When you read today, remember that you *could* use reading workshop time to whip through one book after another after another. But that would mean you'd miss things! So instead, push yourself to sloooow down and reread. Try to see as much as you can on each page!"

Make sure that the text you choose to use in a minilesson is likely to allow or help kids to be successful in their quick try at a new strategy.

ANCHOR CHART

Readers Read
with a Partner

- Sit side by side.
- Put one book in the middle.
- See-saw read.
- Share Wow! pages.
- **Reread to learn more.**

Reread to learn more.

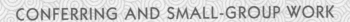

Assessing Concepts of Print and Observing Kids' Reading Behaviors

AS YOU MOVE OUT INTO YOUR WORKSHOP to assess and to support groups of readers, know that rereading is a very important reading behavior. You will want to reinforce this habit in any reader you hear doing it, but you will also want to continue collecting data on your children's concepts about print. To do both, you might break your teacher work during this workshop into two parts.

First, during independent reading, you might move around the room with your Concepts about Print assessment sheet in hand. You began these observations yesterday, so you can work the same way today. Continue to move from table to table watching for, asking about, and checking off boxes for children you did not see yesterday.

Be sure to *teach* as you assess. When a child does not know a concept, show him the concept quickly. Give him the answer. You can check on the child's hold on this information later. Work your way from the earliest concepts to the later concepts as you decide to teach into these. You might say something like "After we read to here," and point to the last word on one line, "then we dip down to this line and read on."

Then, during partner time, you will want to enjoy the opportunity to watch your kids doing all sorts of wild and wonderful things. You will see some readers skip the cover entirely to turn to the first page. When you see that, you might say something like "Hey! You can't do that! You're missing the best way to start a book! The best thing about starting a book is you can figure out what the book will probably be about—and the cover is a huge help. You can't skip the cover!"

This teaching can have even more power if you think about the whole table as you notice and name the strong reading work of individuals and partners. We call this kind of teaching a table conference. During a table conference you can take good work that one child is doing and first compliment that child. After you have said something specific like "I love how you really looked at the cover for a while before turning to the first page," then you will want to call this to the attention of the rest of the children at that table. Remember that a powerful compliment can let your beginning readers know that they have done something in their reading that is worth replicating.

(continues)

MID-WORKSHOP TEACHING
Rereading Means Saying More Words for Each Page

"Eyes here, please. Readers, I just want to remind you to make sure that when you reread, you remember to say *a lot* of words. Some of you are rereading a page in your book, and you are only saying the new thing you see. Rereading means remembering all that you *already* read *and* the new stuff you see on the page.

"So, for example, Joey, who's rereading this page in her book, *Birds and Their Nests*," I held it up so children could see, "might say what she noticed when she *first* read this page. Tell us, Joey."

"The nest is in the grass on the ground," Joey declared.

I continued. "*And* . . . Joey'd add on what she noticed when she *reread*," I said, gesturing for her to share this information.

"The bird's body has black and white dots. And its nest is messy," Joey said.

"Right. So put it all together now," I said. She did, then added, "Hey, that's a lot of words!"

"Yep. Rereading means saying more words about a page."

Reminding Children of the Things Partners Do Together

I called for the students' attention and then I flipped our sign from Private Reading to Partner Reading. I said, "Remember to put your books in a stack between the two of you and then to read them one by one. When you are reading a book together, put the book between the two of you so that you both can look and talk and learn. If you reach a page that you have marked as a Wow! page, be sure you stay on that page for a long time and try to learn all you can from it." I touched each strategy Post-it on our "Readers Read with a Partner" chart as I talked.

A word of caution: after you teach your kids all sorts of things, when you look to see the imprint of your teaching on the kids' behaviors, you will be apt to find no evidence of an impact! (I hope you can imagine the smile on my face. It's the sad truth, but oh, well!) Here is the secret: just keep teaching. Remember that this is how kindergartners learn. They learn and forget. Learn and forget. Use the second part of today's teacher time to move among the kids, helping them do what you have taught so far. Don't be surprised if you are teaching the same few things again and again.

Rereading to Learn from All the Parts of a Page

Take the familiar page students helped you study during the minilesson and cover it almost entirely with Post-it notes, and use the Post-its to illustrate what readers notice when they first read a book compared to when they reread it.

Sitting at the easel, surrounded by kids, I said, "Let's look at the black back beetle page from our book again." I turned the cover toward them so that they could see it.

Then I laid the book in my lap and placed Post-it notes over all the parts of this page except for the antennae and eye. When all Post-its were in place I said, "I want to show you what rereading is helping so many of you do."

I held up the Post-it-covered page for children to see. "On the first read of your book, you only paid attention to a little bit of the page. You maybe only really noticed the one big thing on the page. Like on this page, you maybe only saw the bug's big eye and his long antennae," I said, and pointed to that part of the page, which was uncovered.

I began to remove the Post-it notes, one by one, revealing more of the page. As I did this, I said, "But, when you reread your books, you have a chance to pay attention to more parts of a page. Like on this page, you can read and learn about the legs part of the page, and the back shell part, too—actually, about *all* the parts of the page." I traced my finger slowly over each part of the now Post-it-free page. "Rereading all the parts of the page helps us learn more and then more from our learn-about-the-world books."

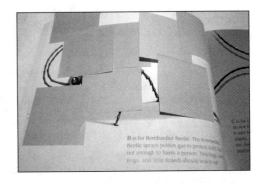

FIG. 5–2 Reading only once can lead to only learning from parts of the page. The Post-its represent the parts we can learn from when we reread.

Readers Reread a Book by Putting All the Pages Together

IN THIS SESSION, you'll teach your readers that rereading also helps you do the work of putting all of the pages together in your book.

GETTING READY

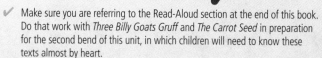

✔ Chart paper for quick-listing children's thoughts (see Connection)

✔ Display "We Are Readers" and "Readers Read with a Partner" charts (see Connection). 👆

✔ Choose a nonfiction demonstration text that you have already read with the class, to practice rereading skills (we use *The Beetle Alphabet Book*, by Jerry Pallotta and David Biedrzycki, also used in Session 2). This should either be a Big Book or a book you can put on the document camera (see Connection, Teaching, Active Engagement, and Share).

✔ Pointers or rulers (see Link)

✔ Private Reading/Partner Reading sign (see Link) 👆

✔ Make sure you are referring to the Read-Aloud section at the end of this book. Do that work with *Three Billy Goats Gruff* and *The Carrot Seed* in preparation for the second bend of this unit, in which children will need to know these texts almost by heart.

MINILESSON

CONNECTION

Marvel with the children at their progress in becoming readers, and ignite their energy around rereading texts to learn even more.

As the sounds of our gathering song grew silent, I began. "You all have become readers. Before my very eyes, in just a few days, children who mostly have had books read *to* them have become children who *read* those books, too!"

I gestured to our anchor charts from the unit so far. "These charts are up here today to remind you of all that you have learned in just a few magical days in our reading workshop. When I say 'Go,' I am wondering if you could turn to your partner and talk about what you have learned so far about reading workshop and about being a reader. Use these charts to help you remember. Ready? Go!"

After about thirty seconds of talk, I called my readers back and I quick-listed what they remembered from the anchor charts. I then planted my finger under *reread* from the chart. "A lot of you talked about the rereading work you did yesterday as readers. Rereading is so important because we can learn more and more from our books when we do this."

I picked up our beetle book, placed it on the easel, and said, "You know how each time you go back to a playground, you often discover something new? Maybe one day it's a worm poking its head in and out of the sandbox and the next day it's an old stump of a tree you've always run right past on your way to the swings."

❖ **Name the teaching point.**

"Today I want to teach you that when you read a book again and again it's just like seeing something new on the playground that you have already been to many times. When you reread a book, you begin to understand some new things about it. One thing you begin to see is that all the pages of a book *go together*. As you read the pages, it's important to put them together with your own words to learn as much as you can."

TEACHING

Demonstrate rereading several pages, using the transition *and then* to link together your reading across the pages.

I turned toward our beetle book. "I want to show you how I do the work of putting the pages together. We have already read some of this book about beetles. When we read the first page, we were so busy paying attention to *this page*, that we really had no time to think about this page *and* the next page. We were so busy learning about the black back beetle, that we did not think about this page together with other pages.

"Okay. So if I am going to think about how the pages go together in my book, I can reread the page, then turn the page, and *as* I am turning the page I am going to try to say some connect-the-pages words. Watch me."

I read from the pictures, "'The letter *b* is for the black back beetle that has long legs, red eyes, and poison that he shoots from his butt.' Did you see me reread the page?"

The kids nodded. Lowering my voice, I said, "Here comes the new part. Watch me. I am going to try to say some connect-the-pages words as I look to the next page." I looked at the next page as I said, "*And then* the letter *c* is for the cucumber beetle."

I made an excited face. "I did it. *And then* were my connect-the-pages words. Watch me do it again."

I read about the cucumber beetle, and as I turned the page, I said, "*And then* the letter *d* is for the poop beetle." (The book said *dung* beetle.) I pointed to the big ball of poop on the page.

"And then," Aiden called.

"Quick-listing" is just a way to quickly jot what kids are sharing. Their words can be jotted down on Post-its or chart paper. It can be a quick method for assessing what parts of your teaching have really stuck with your children. This listing also shows students how much you value what they have to say. You will give this message to them all year, not just when you are quick-listing, but also whenever you take notes about them while you are teaching.

ACTIVE ENGAGEMENT

Invite children to reread more of the text, using transition words in their reading.

I turned to a two-page spread in the book. One page had a picture of a bee, and the other page had a picture of a red June bug.

"Let me give you a quick try at this putting-the-pages-together work. Let's do one all together. First, help me read this page."

"That is a bee, but I don't think bees are beetles," Kevin said.

"Bees have antennae and six legs just like the beetles do," Yamilah added.

Kevin answered, "But, they have sticky-outy wings and the beetles tuck their wings away,"

"Now, let's get ready to turn the page together and use our connecting words. Ready?"

I turned the page and I prompted them all to say, "*And then* . . ." There was a pause as kids reread the page quickly. As they searched the picture, which had a red hard-shell beetle, some of the kids said, "*And then* this is a red beetle with his wings tucked away under his shells. That line is the two sides."

I smiled and said, "Let's try one more time. Remember that after you use your connecting words, you have to look at the new page and remember what you had read before on that page. Do this one with your partner."

After children had read the current page with their partner, I said, "Here we go. Ready?" I turned the page and the kids chorused, "*And then* . . ."

When I heard kids read that this was the page with the *k* bug that has yellow spots and not very long antennae, I called them back to me.

LINK

Send children off to reread their books, reminding them to read using *and then* to connect their reading across multiple pages.

"You all have become such powerful readers. You now know how to connect the pages together when you reread a book. Rereading gives us the chance to think about how the pages of our books go together. How many of you think you might be ready to do that very important *and then* work right now, this very minute, because you are going back to reread a book?"

"*Connecting the pages in a book is one of the most important strategic actions a reader can take. Here we use the very concrete phrase "and then" to help our kids remember that one page of the book goes with another. The truth though is that "and then" is only one very literal way to connect the pages. Connections can also be made with sequence words (such as first, second, third or after that, next, and finally) and by trying to say what you learned so far as you read the picture on the new page. Readers always carry with them what they have learned so far in a book as they read each successive page.*

There were eager hands.

"Remember, when you do this work, that you will need to pause after saying, 'And then' to quickly remember the new page."

I paused and then asked a child to use our pointer to silently tell us what to do next. I helped Riley point to our private reading time sign. And with that, all of my readers were gone, off to their table tubs to read the coolest nonfiction, back to back with their reading partners.

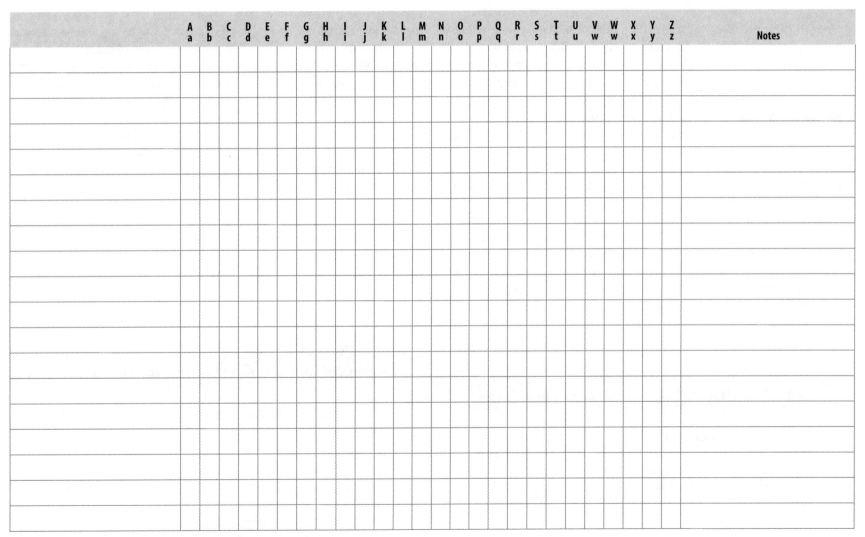

	A a	B b	C c	D d	E e	F f	G g	H h	I i	J j	K k	L l	M m	N n	O o	P p	Q q	R r	S s	T t	U u	V v	W w	X x	Y y	Z z	Notes

FIG. 6–1   A whole-class Letter/Sound data collection record

Supporting Language Development by Encouraging Students to Talk about What They Read

EVEN THOUGH YOU ARE ONLY A FEW DAYS INTO YOUR YEAR, you are probably already noticing children who have come to your kindergarten classroom with few foundational skills. Kindergarten is the grade with perhaps the most difference in the starting points of the kids. Because of this, you must quickly get to know the strengths and needs of your readers so that you can help some children make up for lost ground sooner rather than later. Even though you have already assessed concepts about print and maybe you have checked letter/sound knowledge during writing workshop, the biggest difference you may be noticing between kids is in their talk. While *talk* might not seem to be directly related to *reading*, we should remember what Marie Clay said about language. She said that oral language is the basis of all literacy learning. Another way to say this is that if kids can't say it, then they can't read it or write it.

When kids are reading pages of their learn-about-the-world books, you can hear big differences in the quantity and quality of their words. One thing you might do for children who just say fewer words and less content-specific words is to recycle the book that you use in your minilesson into some quick small-group work to support language development. It will be hard in these first days of workshop to think about pulling together formal small groups. But you might just keep kids for five minutes after your minilesson ends each day and get them reading the pages of this familiar text with you and talking about those pages. When you do this, concentrate on helping these children feel at home with book language and support the sheer quantity of words they say. That means limit the amount of talking *you* do!

Take your vocabulary cues from both the book and the kids. Remember that your kindergarten readers may not yet be able to read these books conventionally, but the closer their talk is to the kinds of words that the book contains, the easier it will be for them to eventually read the book. This concept is true for all books they will read.

One of the great things about a small group such as this is that it is easy. You can work with this small group every day. You might even do this language work after your writing minilesson too. Rest assured that a big investment in oral language now will pay off big later with stronger readers and writers.

MID-WORKSHOP TEACHING **Rereading the Whole Page**

"Readers, eyes up here please. I can see so many of you using your *and then* to connect the pages, but I want to remind you to reread the whole page too. When you reread, you are not only saying, "And then" as you turn the page. You are also rereading the whole page trying to see more and say more on each page. Always, you are doing all of this to learn as much as you can in your learn-about-the-world books."

TRANSITION TO PARTNER TIME
Directing Children to Read and Reread with Partners

I sang from the center of the room, "Stop, look, and listen," and the children joined into the refrain of "Okay!"

Once their eyes were on me, I said, "Readers, it is time for you to work with a partner." I flipped our sign over to the partner side and continued. "I want you to find a book that you reread today and connected the pages inside of. Make sure you start with rereading these books first. Then you can move on to other books that you might read and reread together."

Using Connecting Parts to Do a Quick Retell

Show how you use rereading and connecting pages to retell a book.

As my students settled back on the rug, I said, "It was so cool to watch you put the pages of your learn-about-the-world book together. Rereading is such a powerful thing to do as a reader. There was this sort of extra cool thing that happened when you were connecting pages. I just wanted to show it to you."

I turned back to our beetle book. "When you connect the pages as you reread a book, that work can help you talk about the book in a quick way once you are done. That kind of quick retell about the book is awesome before you start to read or if you are trying to get someone else to read the book that you loved. Or even if you just want to check your reading to help you remember what you are learning. Do you want to see me do a quick retell?"

They all yelled their approval (and even if they don't, I never hear the alternative).

I slowly turned the pages of my book and did the rereading and connecting out loud. For two pages or so I worked just as I had in the minilesson. I then looked up. I wanted to be sure that my students could see the difference between *reading* the book and *retelling* the book. I kept my eyes off the book and said, "My rereading and connecting work can really help me do a quick retell of the book. I paused and shared my thinking here. "Let me remember what I learned so far. I am not sure I remember . . . ' I continued, "So far, there were a lot of different beetle names that began with different letters." I paused and looked up and around to show kids I was trying to remember. I finished, "Also, each beetle has some things the same and some things different."

I looked up. "Did you see that? Because I worked to connect the parts of the book, I could quickly retell you the book. Retelling can be my way to get other people as excited about my book as I am. I think it is so cool that work we are already doing can be used for something else too. Quick retells."

Readers Reread to Rethink

IN THIS SESSION, you'll teach your readers that when they reread a book, they are also learning more because they are rethinking.

GETTING READY

✔ Children will need to bring a book they read and reread yesterday to the rug with them (see Connection).

✔ You will need your demonstration text from yesterday's lesson (we used *The Beetle Alphabet Book*) (see Teaching, Mid-Workshop Teaching, and Share).

✔ Prepare several Post-its with a caricature of yourself to use (see Teaching).

✔ Private Reading/Partner Reading sign (see Link) 👆

✔ Get ready the strategy Post-it "Add a pinch of you." to add to the partnership chart (see Transition to Partner Time). 👆

✔ Make sure you are referring to the Read-Aloud sections at the end of this book. Do that work with *The Three Billy Goats Gruff* and *The Carrot Seed* in preparation for the second bend of this unit, in which children will need to know these texts almost by heart.

MINILESSON

CONNECTION

Give children a moment to practice doing a quick retell about their books.

As the kids came to the rug, they brought a book they had read and reread yesterday. Kids settled down in their rug spots and I said, "Rereading rocks!"

There was silence. I said again, "Rereading rocks! You know why I said that? I was riding home from work yesterday and I was thinking about you guys, and I started to remember watching you reread these books. You were rockin' these books. You are reading books for longer and you are learning more and saying more on each page. When you are rereading, you are connecting the pages, and yesterday you watched me use that rereading and connecting work to quickly retell my book."

I paused. "That quick retell thing. Do you want to try that right now with the book you brought? Right now, would you just turn the pages and do some of your rereading and connecting of the pages work?"

I gave my kids twenty seconds to begin this work.

"Now, when I say, 'Go,' I want you to turn to the person next to you and do a quick retell about the book. Remember, you probably start with words like 'This book is about . . . and it has . . . and it also teaches . . . and there is a page about.' Go!"

For another thirty seconds, my kids did imperfect quick retells. Some were just rereading the book. I was excited because no matter what, they were all rereading with gusto! I silently signaled for them to stop.

"See, readers, rereading rocks. Rereading helps you get more from your learn-about-the-world book. But, rereading isn't *only* about the book. Rereading helps you learn from the books, but it also helps you go beyond the book too!"

Name the teaching point.

"Today I want to teach you that when you read a book again and again, you also have a chance to think more and talk more and learn more. Readers who reread know that rereading means re*thinking*. And rethinking can take you beyond the book."

TEACHING

Demonstrate adding your own thinking when you are rereading, using the words *I think* and inserting a personal connection.

I turned once again to the beetle book and I said, "We have read and reread this book about beetles. We have learned so much about beetles from this book. But once we know a book really well, then we have a chance to reread and add a pinch—that means just a little bit—of our own thinking too! I want to show you how I do that on this first page."

I began to read the page about the fighting beetles. As I started to turn the page, I said, "And then." But I froze the page mid-air; I turned to my students and said, "Oops, I almost forgot to add a pinch of my thinking too!"

I reached for a Post-it on which I had drawn a cartoonish picture of me. I held the Post-it up so that the kids could see it. There were a few giggles. "She's cute," Megan said.

"This is me," I said. "I have to add *me* to each page!" I stuck the Post-it of me onto the page.

I continued. "When I reread the pages in my book, I want to be sure to add in a little bit of me and my thinking to each page. Rereading helps get *me* into the book," and I stuck more Me Post-its onto the page.

"Now that I am on this page," some of the kids giggled, "listen to my rereading. 'Fighting beetles have super short antennae with little balls on the end. They also have antlers like reindeer.' *I think* that they have those hard antlers to fight with and maybe to bite with too. My mom told me that beetles bite when I was little. I always remember that."

Michael called, "I don't think beetles bite, because ladybugs never bite me! I always catch them and they never bite."

In an effort to turn his response to the content of what I said into attention for my teaching point, I said, "Yes. I did add something about biting to this page when I reread it, but I really want you to notice how I said the words *I think*. Those words helped me add a pinch of me to the page."

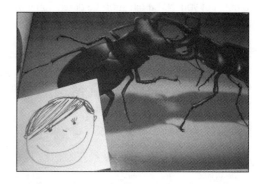

FIG. 7–1 Picture of a "pinch of me" Post-it added to a page to help me remember to say, "I think. . . ."

ACTIVE ENGAGEMENT

Invite children to reread one of their books with a partner, adding a pinch of their own thinking.

"Now, it is your turn, partners. I want one of you to take out your book." Once they had done that I added, "Next, reread a page. Then, just before you turn the page and think about connecting the pages, I want you to add a pinch of you to the page. You can use the words *I think* to help you do that."

The partner with the book began rereading the page to his partner, and I voiced over to no one in particular, "Add a pinch of you now to the page. *I think . . .*"

I listened in as I moved from partnership to partnership.

I coached above the din. "Switch to your partner's book now. Don't forget to reread the page too! Remember, this is a pinch of you. Not a pinch of the *book*. Some of you are doing just a pinch of the book. Big scoops of the book and a pinch of you."

Looking across the rug, I noticed that Dylan and Ruby had somehow gotten Post-its and had quickly drawn cartoonish versions of themselves. And inside Ruby's book, they were busy taking turns adding pinches of their own thinking. Each *I think* was punctuated by a stuck Post-it.

LINK

Send children off to reread, reminding them to add a pinch of *I think*.

I called everyone back together. "Readers, like I said, 'Rereading rocks!' You were adding in the most interesting pinches of you to books that you were rereading. You were making those books rock!"

Holding up two cartoonish faces, I said, "Dylan and Ruby were really helped by having a little face that looked like them, and then when they reread, the face reminded them to try to add a pinch of *I think* before they turned the page. You might make one for yourself today too!"

I sent them off to read with a tap of the Private Reading sign. I could not wait to hear what they were thinking.

It's likely you'll find kids who are naturals at this, who were already adding in their own thinking to these learn-about-the-world books. Their ease with this teaching point should not make you doubt your teaching of this lesson. Especially in kindergarten, children use great strategies and do awesome work without knowing how awesome their work is. If they don't know it is awesome, how will they know to keep doing it? This lesson encourages students to make this inference work part of their regular repertoire.

Your students may or may not have reached for Post-it notes to stick in their books. You might choose to set a partnership up to try this during the active engagement, provisioning them with Post-it notes and pens so they can draw little versions of themselves that you can share with students during the link. Or you might choose to pose this option to students by reminding them of what you did, saying, "I was really helped by having a little face that looked like me. It reminded me to add a pinch of I think before I turned the page. You might make one for yourself today too!"

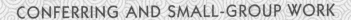
Helping Children Develop Identities as Readers

B Y NOW, you will have learned a lot about what your readers can do and can't yet do. You won't, however, have any formal data for reading affect or for reading identity. These, nevertheless, are central to the work of this unit. Your goal for now is to make a place so that the children in your care grow to love reading and to see themselves as readers. Because these are critically important goals, you might angle your conferring so that you help your children develop identities as readers.

You might want to start with the kids who still seem to be on the fringes of your workshop. Think about which of your kids are just playing with books, which kids use the bathroom every day during reading time, which put their heads down everyday. These might be kids who already harbor a secret belief that they may not be readers.

MID-WORKSHOP TEACHING
Finding Parts of Pages to Back Up Your Thinking

"Stop, look, and listen. Readers, I just want to remind you that when you are adding in what you are thinking on each page, you can really help yourself and your partner understand your ideas better if you find and point to the part of the page that made you think what you thought."

Pointing at the beetle book, I continued, "Nivaeh did that for me in our *Beetle Alphabet Book*. When she said she thought poop beetles rolled poop into balls to lay eggs on them so their babies could eat, she then pointed to the part of the picture that showed the beetle sitting on top of the poop ball. She then said, 'See her on the ball? I think she is there laying eggs, and we just can't see them because they are under her.'

"Don't forget to point to the page or the place on a page that could help people understand your *I think*, your pinch of you."

If you have some of these kids, don't spend too much time trying to get them to talk about their reasons for resisting reading. Instead, do something about this. Ask them, "What do you love most in the world?" Then get them talking about their love. Listen as they light up and observe their feelings. After you've seen that, you have your goal.

(continues)

TRANSITION TO PARTNER TIME   Channeling Partners to Read Together and Add Their Own Thoughts

"Readers. Eyes, please. It is almost time for partner reading. Today is an especially exciting day. You have the chance now to put your book in the middle and reread and then add in a pinch of you to each page. Don't forget that with a partner in your book, you can add in at least *two* pinches of *I think* to each page. Because there are two of you, each book will get an extra boost of thinking during partner reading time." I added the strategy Post-it "Add a pinch of you." to our anchor chart.

ANCHOR CHART

Readers Read with a Partner

- Sit side by side.
- Put one book in the middle.
- See-saw read.
- Share Wow! pages.
- Reread to learn more.
- **Add a pinch of you.**

I think...

Add a pinch of you.

Either that day or the next day, your goal is to make reading attractive enough for this child that he lights up when talking about reading too. Go find books on these children's favorite topics. Send books home for these children to read with their favorite people. Bring the books these kids are reading front and center in your minilessons.

When kids feel badly about reading, again, instead of haggling about this, try to reverse their feelings by making reading into tremendous fun.

Above all, on this day of your unit, don't forget the kids who are on the fringes. They need you more than anyone.

By the way, finding out what **every** child loves most in the world will help you teach your entire class in the most powerful ways.

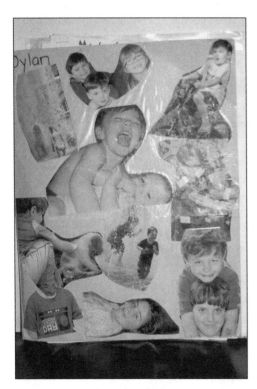

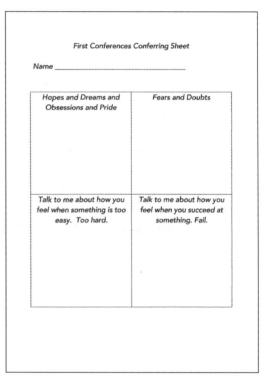

FIG. 7–2   Tools to help you get to know your students better: a decorated writing folder, Map of the Heart, and First Conference Conferring Sheet

Readers Think Widely about How to Add a Pinch of Themselves to the Pages

Point out that one way to have thoughts about your reading is to let the text remind you of something—a movie, another book, even stuff from other people.

At the rug again, I said, "You all were adding in pinches of you all over the room. It is so interesting to read the book and learn from the book, and it feels so good to reread trying to connect the pages. Now, we have this new thing—adding in our *I thinks* when we reread too."

I paused to change course a little in my teaching. "I wanted to share with you one tip for making your *I thinks* even better. I showed you already how you can point to the page to help someone understand your thinking—like Nivaeh. I also wanted to tell you another tip. Ready?"

A bunch of eyes looked up. "It is this. Your little pinch of *you* on each page doesn't have to only come from just *you* or your partners."

"What?" a few kids said.

"You may get to a page, and while you are rereading it, you may feel like you are not thinking anything. You may be worried that there is no pinch of you to add to the page. But I want to tell you that you can add stuff from other places too. Other books or movies, shows, or other people can help you add some extra thinking to a page."

I turned to the spider page in our beetle book. "That happened to me here. I tried to say, 'I think,' but I had nothing to say. Then, I remembered a show I saw once with spiders. On that show they said that spiders are not insects because they have too many legs and they don't have wings. On this page, the stuff from the show was the pinch of me that I added when I reread this page.

"Cool, right?! You might remember this tip—that the pinch you add to a page can come from lots of places—the next time you are rereading to rethink."

Learning how to stop and think while reading is one of the most important reading habits. Using the text to grow a thought is how kids make inferences. While we have emphasized saying, "I think . . ." and "I remember from somewhere else . . ." to help kids have thoughts that push them beyond the text, you will want to model a range of inference strategies. In the very beginning, the illustrations are often the source of ideas in a book. Teaching kids how to put parts of a page or a book together can help them make inferences too!

Rereading Helps Readers Learn from Words in Books, Too

IN THIS SESSION, you'll teach students that reading both the pictures and the words on each page will help them learn more in each book.

GETTING READY

✔ Use a familiar information book that has close-up photographs and familiar vocabulary (we use *The Beetle Alphabet Book*) for your demonstration of how to study the words in a book (see Teaching) and for children's practice (see and Active Engagement).

✔ "Readers LEARN from Books, Too!" anchor chart and new strategy Post-its—"We learn from pictures." "We learn from words." (see Connection and Link)

✔ Have a photo of a place in the school that you read during Session 1's minilesson to remind students of their earlier work (see Teaching).

✔ Dry erase marker and small Post-its (see Active Engagement)

✔ "Readers Read with a Partner" anchor chart and the strategy Post-it "Read the pictures and the words." (see Transition to Partner Time)

✔ Make sure you are referring to the Read-Aloud section at the end of this book. Do that work with *The Three Billy Goats Gruff* and *The Carrot Seed* in preparation for the second bend of this unit, in which children will need to know these texts almost by heart.

MINILESSON

CONNECTION

Point out that people learn about the world through books, then orchestrate children to select one thing they learned and to say it aloud in unison, creating a drumroll for your teaching.

"Readers, one of the great things about reading is that you learn about the world. Think of one thing you have learned from reading. You got that one thing in your mind?" I waited a minute. "Right now, in your mind, say what you learned as a sentence. 'I learned that . . .' Like I might say from reading our Beetle book, 'I learnd there is a beetle that eats poop.'"

"Okay, now the challenge is when I say, 'three,' you are *all* going to say what you learned out into the air so that this room is full of all your learning. Do you need to practice for a minute? To practice, whisper into your hand, saying one thing you learned. Whisper, 'I learned . . .'"

After they did this, I said, "So on the count of three, everyone will say what you learned into the air, so our room gets filled with it. You ready? One, two, three!"

The children all spoke at once, creating a rousing noise.

I gave them a thumbs up. "Because you learned so many new, exciting, and different things about the world from your books, I can tell you studied the pictures really closely to learn from them!"

❖ **Name the teaching point.**

"Today I want to teach you that as you read books again and again, you really do see new things each time you reread. You also start to notice the *words* more and more. You can read the words in a book like you read the words in the classroom, and in the school. You see the words, and you think, think, think, to figure out what they probably say."

TEACHING

Explain how you can study the words in a book, as children earlier studied environmental print, using the pictures to figure out what the words might say.

"Do you remember how on the first day of reading workshop you read the school? You all looked at words like this one." I held up a photo of the front office, capped with the label "Main Office." "And you thought, 'What could that say?' and looked for hints, and you figured out what it said. You can do the same thing when you read your books. You can find words on the page and figure out what they say.

"Let me show you how I do that in our beetle book." I turned to the letter *p* page with the pie dish beetle.

"When I was sitting with a few of you yesterday, we read this *p* page by looking at the pictures and saying as much as we could about the whole page. But because we have been rereading our books again and again, we realized that we could also probably read some of the actual *words* on this page. We had not really tried to read the *words* before."

I paused and Riley jumped in, "That's maybe 'cause there are a lot of words on that page."

"There are a lot of words, but you know how to do this thing where you study the picture and then say words that go with the picture and then look at the words. When you look at the words, you can think, think, think. You can ask yourself, 'Do I see any words that match what I said on this page?'"

Remembering Riley's comment, I said, "There are a lot of words on the page, but we are not trying to read all of the words. But, maybe some."

Conduct a think-aloud using a page from the demonstration text, first reading the picture closely and then searching the page to find the words you read.

I demonstrated by doing a think-aloud. "This page has the letter *p*, and the shape of the beetle looks really round on the letter *p* right here. I am not really sure what his /p/ sounding name is but I know he is a round beetle." Musing to myself, I continued, "This is a round beetle kind of like the Mexican yellow ladybug beetle. Hmm, . . . I keep saying the word *beetle*. Now, I can do one more rereading thing. I can search the page to see if the word *beetle*, the word I keep repeating, might be on the page."

I looked at the *p* page. "Let's see. Let's see. *Beetle, beetle,*" I mused as I now moved my finger under the words. I continued to chant, "*Beetle, beetle,*" and then I said, "I think /b/ is the letter *b*. Oh, wait here. Here is a letter *b*. I think this might say, 'beetle.'"

What you want here is a page that might be easy to read because it has close-up photographs, has vocabulary that kids probably already use when they talk, and has words that show up in more than one place on the page.

This teaching point can be tricky because you do not want children with low knowledge about letter/sound correspondence to think that they are decoding words on the page. In other words, if a child knows almost no letter/sounds, then you do not want them to think that they are suddenly being asked to use their letter/sound knowledge to read or decode words. You want them to use the pictures and their language to help them see a word or two on the page. They will probably only be able to read words correctly if they also know the letter and the sound that particular word starts with. They are really only reading words because of the number of times they have reread a particular book. Children usually see the first letter of a word as they begin to look at words.

The kids were all cheering me on. I continued to look for the word *beetle* on the page. We found it a bunch more times.

Debrief. Name the transferable steps you took.

I continued, "Did you see how I read some of the words? I looked carefully at the picture and then said words that went with the picture, and then I searched for words with letters that matched what I said. We read *beetle* this way."

ACTIVE ENGAGEMENT

Invite children to try this work on another page in the demonstration text, first rereading the page by studying the picture, then searching for the words they said on the page.

"Now it is your turn. I want you to give this word reading a try on the spider page that we looked at before. First, can you look carefully at the picture and reread this page with your partner?" I gave students a minute to do this. "I heard you all say, 'Spider'! With your partner, I want you to keep saying, 'Spider, spider,' as you look at the words on the page up here and trace your finger in the air. Decide what sound then letter you think that word might start with and then see if you can find a word with that starting letter."

Support all students in reading words by connecting the word, sound, and letter. Encourage students to search for the word in other places on the page.

After about one minute of varying degrees of word-reading success, I decided to help them all be successful at finding the word.

I said, "Let's practice how we read words during rereading together right now. So on this page you all kept saying the word *spider* because we know that's what this page teaches. Then, you heard a sound at the start of the word. Many of you heard the /s/ sound. /S/, /s/, spider."

Reaching for a dry erase marker and a Post-it, I added, "Then some of you knew that the letter *s*," and I wrote that letter on the Post-it, "makes the /s/ sound. This is the letter *s*." I then stuck the Post-it under the lines that had the word *spider* in them. I knew this proximity would support kids as they searched for the word.

"Now that we think we know what a word might look like, we can search for that word on the page. A few of you saw the word *spider* here with the big *s*," and I pointed under it. "But can we find that word anywhere else? This whole page does teach us about a spider. That word might be on the page again."

I was silent for a few seconds, and then together we found the word *spider* in two more places on the page.

As partners begin chanting and trying to hear an initial sound, be on the lookout for kids at various stages of development. Some kids will have the phonemic awareness to hear the initial sound, and they might know the name of the letter that makes that sound, but they might not remember what that letter looks like. Other children will be able to hear the sound but not know a letter that makes that sound. A third group will know the sound, name, and look of the letter. And one last group might not be able to do any of this phonemic awareness/phonics work at all.

Remember that active engagements are a great time for assessment, and this particular work children are doing will provide much data.

LINK

Remind children that they can learn from all parts of a book—the pictures and the words—by rereading pages and searching for words they can reread.

Not wanting to lose the excitement that was generated by finding more words we could read, I rushed to the end of my minilesson so that they could go read. "So, readers, remember that you can use all the parts of the book to learn about the world." I tapped the bullet on the chart. "We can learn from the pictures."

I moved to the last bullet on the chart. "*And* we can learn from the words. Remember that when we reread our books, we can start to notice and read some of the words. Use what you saw and what you said on the page to help you search for words that you might be able to read."

I gestured toward the chart once more. "Thumbs up if you're going to practice this reading work today with your own books! Amazing! Off you go!"

Helping Kids With Beginning Word Reading

1. Study the picture and say what it teaches. Be sure to add a pinch of you.

2. Listen for repeating words as you read a page.

3. Say one of those words again and again.

4. Listen for the first sound and try to remember the letter that makes that sound. (an alphabet chart can help)

5. Search the words for a word that starts with the letter.

6. Try to find that word many times on the page.

Meeting Children Where They Are

Welcome Approximations and Conventional Reading, and Assess

LET'S FACE IT. You will probably have more than a few kids who can't read much of anything in a conventional way quite yet. The thing to remember is that when babies learn to talk, they gurgle and blab, and parents talk back to them, as if in a dialogue. Kids learn to walk that way, too. They stand, stumble, cruise along the sofa, and parents announce, "She's walking!" For most kids, today's session is an invitation—even a nudge—for kids to approximate. Although talking about the book and reading the pictures is a great way to be engaged with texts, there is also a place for working with print, trying to decode it, drawing on as much meaning as possible, as well as on any knowledge one has about letters and sounds.

MID-WORKSHOP TEACHING
Reinforcing Children's Efforts to Read Pictures and Words

"Hey, readers, give me your eyes, please. I see so many of you looking for words that you can read. You are searching the pages carefully for words and finding words everywhere. Hold up your finger for how many words you found that you could read." I took a few seconds to name out the numbers I saw. "I just wanted to remind you that you also want to continue to do the work of studying and then reading the whole page. Reading both the pictures *and* the words on the page will help you learn the most that you can from every book."

Any nudging might involve *you* pointing out letters and words on a page. This kind of work will go better if you follow the lead of your readers. For instance, if a child is obsessing about the dolphin on a page, then you might point out how the word *dolphin* starts with the /d/ sound. You might then show the child the word *dolphin*. You could then also connect the /d/ sound to the letter *d*. For your nonconventional readers, even a little bit of work like this will help them know how the word work from other parts of the day connects with their reading of books.

Background knowledge matters so much too. You want your readers to use what they already know to help them read books. You could model for them how you will often say things like "I already know . . ." or "I read in another book . . ." or "I saw on a show once . . . ," and then you go to read the page. As you taught students yesterday, we always want kids to bring all that they know to every text that they read.

Then, too, you are apt to find that, in fact, some of your kids have come to your classroom reading and are entirely able to decipher labels and some captions in their nonfiction books. By nudging kids to read the words as best they can, you give yourself an important opportunity to assess. And you never want your teaching to make kids feel like they should do *less* than they know how to do! Remember that writing workshop will also help you know who has what knowledge about letters and sounds. If a child is labeling in writing using first and last letters, then they should be able to read words in their books using that same knowledge. These kids may need you to show them how you use letter/sound knowledge and thinking together to read words in the book.

Channeling Partners to Read the Pictures and Words Together

Standing next to the "Readers Read with a Partner" chart, I said, "As you move to sitting side by side, book in the middle, reading and then talking, I want you to remember that you can also read the *words* together now too! Remember to read the pictures and talk together and point to the words to try reading some of them together." I added the Post-it to the chart.

As I moved around the room, I continued to finish up my concepts about print assessment. I also observed and named positive partner behaviors, knowing that my constant reinforcement would help my students use reading workshop in more and more powerful ways. I was also on the lookout for kids who might be part of my share.

ANCHOR
CHART

Readers Read with a Partner

- Sit side by side.
- Put one book in the middle.
- See-saw read.
- Share Wow! pages.
- Reread to learn more.
- Add a pinch of you.
- **Read the pictures and the words.**

Read the pictures and the words.

Highlighting Partner Work that Supports Word Reading

Share how talking and reading with a partner can also help you read some of the words in your book.

"Readers, the coolest thing was happening when you were reading and talking about your books today. Many of you had found a word or two that you could read when you were reading during private reading, and you shared those words with your partner during partner reading. But the really cool thing was that as you read and talked with your partner, you were sometimes able to read even more words!"

Looking out at the class, I saw *some* nods, but the truth is that I did not expect a lot of nodding. Reading the words in a book is not really an expectation in this first unit for kindergarten. However, I wanted to be sure to invite my readers to try to at least look at the words, especially when they are rereading their books.

To make my word-looking invitation even more memorable, I added, "When Megan and Matthew were reading together, they were on this page." I held up a close-up picture of a dolphin flying from the water.

"On this page, Megan had already found the word *dolphin*, and she and Matthew were reading that word wherever they saw it. But, as they talked, Matthew said that the waves were really high in the picture and then he said that he thought he saw the word *waves*. He and Megan searched for that word and they found it right here."

I pointed to the word *water*. Remember that these two had done the word-reading work that we had practiced so far, saying-hearing-finding the first letter, even though they had not read the word accurately. And the words could have been waves. There are waves in water. His miscue made sense, which is a big deal in reading. Here I celebrated their approximation.

"Readers, did you see how talking and thinking and looking together as partners got them another word they could read? Maybe you all could try that tomorrow!"

Readers Sound Like Teachers When They Read Learn-about-the-World Books

MINILESSON

In the connection, you will probably want to remind your readers of how they are reading so much more on each page by making sure that they see the whole page. You might also remind and maybe even show them how you took careful notes on what they were saying as they read their books yesterday.

You might lead to your teaching point by saying something like, "Yesterday I noticed that *what* you were saying was getting more and more powerful, but I also noticed that *how* you were reading did not sound quite right."

For the teaching point you could say, "Today I want to teach you that when you read a learn-about-the-world book again and again, you can begin to make the book sound right. Learn-about-the-world books teach, and so they sound like a teacher. When you read these books again and again, one thing you are trying to do is to sound like a teacher too."

Add a new Post-it to the chart.

ANCHOR CHART

Readers LEARN from Books, Too!

- We learn from pictures.
- We learn from words.
- **We sound like a teacher.**

We sound like a teacher.

During your teaching, you might read aloud some tiny excerpts from several nonfiction books, accentuating the authoritative voice. Then you could contrast this sort of reading with an exaggerated role-play that shows how *not* to read nonfiction.

When you do the authoritative reading of your nonfiction, you will want to take on a professorial attitude, perhaps sitting up a little straighter and adjusting your glasses for emphasis.

During the active engagement, channel kids to try reading the next page of their book, reading it first *not* as teachers might, and then revising their voices and posture to read it with the voice of a teacher. Listen for children who are not getting the difference between the two kinds of reading.

You might offer some help by saying, "Learn-about-the-world books say things like 'I have something to teach you, so listen up,' or 'There are three things to know about this. First . . .' When you read these books you need to sound like someone who really knows—a scientist, an expert, a teacher."

In your link, remind kids of all that they have learned to do so far as readers. You might talk through your anchor chart to do that reminding work.

CONFERRING AND SMALL-GROUP WORK

As you confer and pull small groups today, support students in drawing on a repertoire of reading strategies. If you see students reading the pictures closely, compliment this and remind them also to read the words. If you see students reading the pictures and the words, celebrate this while also reminding them to add a pinch of themselves to every page.

Mid-Workshop Teaching

In your mid-workshop teaching, it's likely you'll hear students slipping away from reading like a teacher, so you might highlight a student who noticed she wasn't reading with a teaching voice and then caught herself and reread so she sounded like a teacher. Remind students that they can do the same.

Transition to Partner Time

Partnerships can listen to each other read and remind each other especially about the importance of reading like a teacher. As they are working together, you can point out how good it is to reread a part if it does not sound right. The first time you read a page it often sounds more tentative, but then they should reread. Be sure also to remind your partners to read and then *talk* about their books.

SHARE

Today's share session can involve admiring the sounds of nonfiction books. You might conduct an imaginary orchestra of professorial-sounding learn-about-the-world book readers. You could say, "When I tap you with my baton, will you read a page of your book to us? And class, let's listen to the sounds of these learn-about-the-world books."

FIG. 9–1   This writing is typical of kindergarten at this time of the year.

Readers Can Read Stories They Have Heard a Zillion Times

IN THIS SESSION, you'll teach your students how to turn stories that have been read to them a zillion times into stories they can read on their own.

GETTING READY

✔ Be prepared to refer to the "We Are Gathering" song lyrics (see Connection). ✋

✔ Prepare familiar books (old favorite storybooks), wrapped like presents, that you can unwrap with your students to build excitement about the new texts they will be reading in the new bend. These can be used books, which you will put into table tubs after this lesson. See a list of recommended title on the online resources (see Connection). ✋

✔ Gather your charts from Bend I so that children can read them and can continue to recall what they've learned (see Connection and Share). ✋

✔ Place the anchor chart "We Are Storybook Readers!" on the easel and have the first strategy Post-it ready—"Look at the pictures, remember, read!" (see Connection and Share). ✋

✔ Have a familiar emergent storybook you've read aloud several times ready to use. We suggest *The Three Billy Goats Gruff* (see Teaching and Active Engagement).

✔ Have ready the Stages of Emergent Storybook Reading document (see Conferring and Small-Group Work) ✋

✔ Private Reading/Partner Reading sign (see Transition to Partner Reading) ✋

✔ Prepare a second bin of books, filled with learn-about-the-world books, that children will pull from during the share. You may want to tuck these bins out of sight and place them on tables during your transition to learn-about-the-world reading, or you may choose to designate a student leader to switch the bins (see Share).

MINILESSON

CONNECTION

Celebrate the growth you saw in readers during Bend I. Showcase that growth by asking them to look at something in the room they can read.

I stood beside the easel and began to sing the class gathering song, gesturing for the children to join me in the meeting area. The children chimed in, singing along, as I reminded a few students of their correct spots on the rug. Once everyone had settled, I began.

"Has any grown-up ever said to you, 'My, you've grown so fast!'? Well, you have been growing as readers. On the first day of school, I watched you read your way around the building, and then I watched as you made your first tries at reading alone and together with a partner, and lately, I have watched you reading learn-about-the-world books, learning so much on every page. Now many of you are even finding things to read in your homes and in your neighborhoods—and even right here in this classroom. Right now, with your eyes, eye-point to one thing in this classroom that you can read!"

I demonstrated, giving a laser stare at the words of our gathering song. Then they did a similar point. I turned my head toward different parts of the room to signal all the places where they might be able to read. I pointed to our anchor charts at the front of the room. I then said, "That's right. We are surrounded by things you can read."

Give each child a wrapped familiar story that they will share with other kids at their table.

"You have grown so much as readers, and so today, I want to add one more thing to the list of things you can read."

I reached behind the easel, pulled out a box of wrapped books, and held a few up so children could see.

"Ooh, presents," they cooed.

"Yes, these are presents. These presents belong to all of us." I handed one to each student, reading off the name tags I had affixed earlier to be sure that each table tub would get at least one copy of each title at the end of the minilesson.

"When I count to three, I want you to open your presents. One, two, three!"

After the paper flinging and excited cries subsided, I said, "Some of these presents are the old favorite storybooks that you have been hearing me read aloud to you since the first days of school. Others are books that will become old favorites soon."

As kids began to call out the titles, I interjected, calling on specific children so that the whole class would know what books were in the mix. When a child said the name of his book, I then asked, "Who else has that book?" Once all the calls of "I do!" died down, I said, "Hold your book up in the air.

"Readers, these old favorite storybooks will now be a part of our table tubs and a part of our reading time. You now have two kinds of books you can read every day. Learn-about-the-world books *and* old favorite storybooks.

"Before you go back to read, I want to make sure you know what to do with these books now that you are in charge of reading them."

❧ Name the teaching point.

"Today I want to teach you that when you have heard a story a zillion times, you can practically read it all by yourself. You look at the picture, remember how the story goes, and then read it to yourself, page by page."

I started the new anchor chart:

ANCHOR CHART

We Are Storybook Readers!

- We look at the pictures, remember, read!

Before you start this minilesson, you will need to wrap some of your classroom books as presents that your students can unwrap in anticipation for the new bend. Instead of wrapping up new books, you'll ideally wrap up the old favorites you've been sharing with students through your read-alouds since Day One of school. Unwrapping the gift of old favorite storybooks will ignite the children's excitement around this new work. And wrapping up used books for your children to unwrap is, in fact, how you will get them into table tubs for use in the remainder of the unit.

Depending on how much read-aloud time you have been able to fit into your days, and considering that you will want to have read each title three to five times before you give them to children, by this time in the unit you probably have three or four different titles wrapped up for this lesson.

You might choose to strategically distribute the wrapped texts to groups of students, based on your initial assessments in Bend I. For example, you could give copies of the new demonstration text, The Three Billy Goats Gruff, to children with the least developed oral language, because your repeated use of the text within minilessons will provide them with a little extra support as they take on this new kind of reading.

TEACHING

Demonstrate how to read an emergent storybook. First, show students how you read aloud the title, look over the page, and recall the story.

Picking up *The Three Billy Goats Gruff*, I said, "In a minute I'll show you what the reading of an old favorite storybook looks like, but before I do, would you take your present and sit on it, please?"

Once all kids were sitting on their books, I said, "You will be able to read this story all by yourselves." Some faces looked more confident than others did. "You will be able to read these books all by yourself because you have heard these books over and over again." To the still doubting faces I said, "Really!"

Holding up the book, I said, "Watch how I first look at the pictures and remember how the story goes." I studied the picture on the cover and read the title out loud. Then I turned to the first page.

Pointing to the picture, I demonstrated looking at the picture and remembering the story. "I see the three goats on this page, and one is eating grass. These are the big and medium and small Billy Goats Gruff."

Stepping out of the role of reader and back to my teacher role, I leaned forward to the kids and said, "See how I look at the picture and say what I see? I also try to remember the story when I do this. I think about all the times I have heard this story."

Likely, you've been using The Three Billy Goats Gruff *and* The Carrot Seed *as emergent storybook read-alouds. You may be surprised to note that* The Three Billy Goats Gruff *is the more supported, easier book for students to do this emergent reading work in. This may seem counterintuitive because* The Carrot Seed *has far fewer words on a page. But remember, this is not yet about reading the words. This is about approximating reading, getting a handle on literary language and how stories go. Just as you directed some students to* The Three Billy Goats Gruff, *some kids will be channeled to* The Carrot Seed, *probably because they have more letter/sound knowledge, and their approximated reading will come closer to reading the words.*

Show students how you read the book by saying the words you think could be written on the page. They will be approximations of the actual words, and with repeated readings will become closer to the text.

Turning back to the cover, I said, "Now, let me show you how I read from the beginning." Then, I started my role-played reading by reading the title, "The Three Billy Goats Gruff," in a big, clear voice. I turned the page.

There were three goats, and they were all called the Billy Goats Gruff. The big one ate grass, and there was a middle and small one.

Shift between the role of reader and the role of teacher, making very clear from your posture and voice when you are "reading" the book and when you are debriefing on what you just did.

Looking up at the children I said, "You see?! I am reading it."

Once upon a time there were three Billy Goats. They lived in a valley and the name of all three Billy Goats was "Gruff."

5

Turning to the next page. I said, "Watch me do it again. I will look at the picture and remember the story, and then I will read."

I placed my finger on the picture and thought out loud. "I see the three goats, and the middle one's tongue is out. They are hungry and they want to go up on that hill to get food to get fat."

Looking up I said, "Okay, now let me *read* it."

> *There was very little grass in the valley and the Billy Goats were hungry. They wanted to go up the hillside to a fine meadow full of grass and daisies where they could eat and eat and eat, and get fat.*

ACTIVE ENGAGEMENT

Invite children to try the next page with you, first studying the picture to remember the story and then reading the page with a partner.

"Let's try the next page together. First, let's look at it to remember what happens in this part of the story and say what we see." I got us started with "I see a bridge and . . . ," then gestured for the children to chime in.

"A troll!" several kids shouted.

"Remember what is happening in the story," I coaxed.

I got us started with, "The goats wanted to go over the bridge but . . ."

Liam said, "A big ugly troll lived under it and he was really nasty. He said, 'Who's that?'"

"Good!" I recruited the class to join together in a *reading* of that page.

Return to the beginning of the text, and ask students to remember and then read several pages with a partner.

"Now try reading all the pages we just read with your partner. I'll turn the pages. You all look at the pictures, remember the story, and then read the page together." I returned to the title, showed it, and let kids read it aloud with their partner. Then I turned to the first page, and they continued.

As partners worked together, I coached into their reading. Rather than worrying about the exact words they said, I instead praised their use of the strategy—looking at the page, remembering the story, saying more—so that they would know what I valued most in their reading. In their case, I wanted to be sure that I valued their approximations.

Shifting between retelling the page and the story, to storytelling them, is crucial to the growth of your readers. In this second part of the unit, you are teaching your kids how books sound. Storybooks don't "talk like" list books or learn-about-the-world books.

You can also support the development of a storytelling voice by devoting 5–10 minutes a day to talk practice. In many kindergarten classrooms teachers schedule this time after lunch and call it Storytelling Time. One way this time might go to develop narrative skills is to have kids storytell the events of their lives. They can do this work both in school and at home. Coach and model for kids how you make your own true stories sound like the Old Favorites you have been reading. Help your kids see that your stories do not sound like list books or learn-about-the-world books.

LINK

Remind children to use the pictures and their knowledge of the story to read their old favorites, and then send them off with their new books to begin reading.

"Turn back," I said softly. Most children kept reading with their partner. I repeated softly, "Turn back." As most children turned, I held up two fingers and said, "It took me two times to get your attention. That was pretty good actually, with all of the noise of your reading work. But I am wondering if you could turn back with only *one* signal from me. Next time, keep your ears open for my direction."

Shifting gears, I held up *The Three Billy Goats Gruff* and flipped through the first few pages. "You all know how to read an old favorite storybook now. You can look at the pictures and remember the story and then read." I pointed to the visuals on the chart. "You are ready to read some of these books on your own. Right now, take out the book you're sitting on, place it in your lap, and sit up nice and tall so I know you're ready to head back to your seat. Start by reading the book I gave you, and then you can read from the bin at the center of your table. There will be other old favorite storybooks there. Remember that these books belong to all of us, so when you are finished with the book you unwrapped, put it in the table tub, so that others can read it, and pick another book."

I sent them off.

Energizing Students around Old Favorite Storybook Reading

THIS BEND BEGINS A NEW KIND OF READING WORK, so a good chunk of your time today will be spent rallying students to this new work. That is, you'll need to move quickly among your kids, helping as many of them as possible engage in this new work. Move quickly among students, planting seeds of excitement as you read side by side with children. "This is such a beautiful book," you will whisper to one student as he tentatively holds it out. "I can't wait to hear you read it."

As this unit begins, carefully observe to see what your students can already do as emergent storybook readers. A researcher named Elizabeth Sulzby has articulated stages of development that you are apt to see, all occurring before readers read conventionally, and you'll find a document, Stages of Emergent Storybook Reading, detailing Sulzby's stages of emergent storybook development as part of the online resources. According to Sulzby, the power of this kind of reading comes as much from the implicit teaching that happens when you're side by side with a child who is reading as from the explicit teaching that happens when you teach a whole-class minilesson—or a group of children.

Because of this, conferring in this unit will feel different from conferring in other units of study. This bend is all about getting students to believe they are readers, to become readers, and to achieve this goal we recommend limiting the explicit talk you **do** with students about their reading strategies. You want to get students to do reading, not to spend their time **talking about** the reading work they're doing. Therefore, you will want to watch the level of explicitness with which you teach reading strategies in these books. Sulzby's research showed that kids at home do almost no talking about strategies when they are doing this kind of reading with loved ones. You'll work to replicate these experiences for your students in school. As you do this work, remember that time spent gathered around a book with a child is tremendously powerful.

The kind of conferring you'll do in this bend need not be tricky, it's just different. It can be helpful, as kids are first reading their old favorite storybooks, to do two things. First, watch and listen carefully to the reader. Take notes on what he is saying as he reads. Watch carefully what he notices from the picture, and study the actual words a bit to see what he is getting and not getting.

Then, it is your turn to make a conferring move. You have two choices in this moment. If a child is mostly getting the story and has a little reading swagger and has also begun to use more of the book language, then you might choose to react emotionally. Laugh at funny parts the child reads, or model confusion and comment back to the text. Be careful that you are modeling your true reactions; authenticity can be felt, and it is incredibly useful for new readers to see and be able to copy this behavior. An authentic reaction gives your beginning reader a vision, right from the start, of what it means to read. Reading is understanding. People choose to read and people love to read because it causes reactions. Reading is worthwhile because it moves us all to action.

Or, in this conferring moment, you might choose a second option. If a child is reading only parts of the text but is also missing parts, and if the child is still using everyday language, you could take over the reading of a page of the book. You do not need to

(continues)

MID-WORKSHOP TEACHING   Reading the Pages in Order

I called, "Stop, look, and listen," and the kids responded, "Okay!"

"Readers, I have a big 'Oops' to share with you right now. I heard some of you saying 'Oops' to yourself because you forgot to read each . . . page . . . one . . . by . . . one. I'm so glad you realized this was a problem. I want to remind you that you can't . . . skip . . . pages. If you skip pages, that big brother billy goat may never get to cross the bridge! The boy might never plant his carrot seed! You can't skip pages, or the story won't happen the way it's supposed to! Back to your books, but beware of skipping pages."

After calling children's attention and flipping our sign from Private Reading to Partner Reading, I said, "It's time to read your old favorite storybook with a partner! Remember what you already know about partner reading. Put the book in the middle and take turns see-saw reading.

"Also, I want you to really listen to each other. Really listen to your partner, because even though you have heard these books many times and even though you will read them on your own a lot, your partner will still probably use different words than you do, or he might remember a part that you keep forgetting. Try to listen so that you can get better by doing what you do *and then adding in* what your partner does, too."

talk about *how* you read that page. Instead, simply read the page and then invite the child to read the page using your words right after you do it. "I did it. Now it's your turn," you might say. You can repeat this for a few more pages to help a child build momentum in the book.

You can use this work to support students who are looking at pages but not saying any words; read the page, then invite the child to read after you. Or you might support children who are only naming things they see in pictures by highlighting with your voice what is happening on the page, too. Of course, you're also likely to see children turning pages quickly and saying almost nothing on each page. Show these children how you put your finger on the page and use it to explore the entire picture, reading everything you touch. Invite the child to take over the pointing and reading after you take a turn. If the reading is better, say, "Good! Keep going like that!" If the reading is not better, do not rush straight to explicit strategy naming. Instead, demonstrate reading another page, using your finger to help. In this unit, we want our kindergarteners to copy what we do, not necessarily repeat back what we teach.

You can also use the shared reading move of asking kids to join in with you as you reread parts. They won't actually be reading these parts. It will sound more like singing, with both of you saying the parts together.

Transitioning the Class to Learn-about-the-World Reading

Channel children to read their learn-about-the-world books from Bend I.

Instead of calling the children to the rug, I called to them at their seats. "Readers, we have ten more minutes of reading time, and some of you have been *begging* for the chance to read your learn-about-the-world books. So instead of coming to the rug for share, get a learn-about-the-world book from your table tub."

I paused for ten seconds as I made sure kids knew which books to pick. Then I hung the "Readers LEARN from Books, Too!" chart from the first bend over the "We Are Storybook Readers!" chart for this bend and said, "Readers, remember the work we did to read these books well? Here is the chart to remind you. Show me your learn-about-the-world muscles. Ready to use those muscles? Go!"

After your kids have read for another ten minutes or so, you will want to move your readers back to the rug for another read-aloud or a shared reading. As you begin either of these balanced literacy components, you will want to make explicit the connections between this work and your reading workshop work.

You might also use this time to do some interactive writing. You could make some class books. These books are great ways to build community, and they will also become texts that you will use in the second unit. The topic of these books should be of high interest to your class. Titles like "Things Our Class Likes to Do," "Things Our Class Likes to Eat," and "Things Our Class Likes to Play" often lead to books that your class will be super excited to read again and again.

Because this will be the first time your children are reading from two collections of books, from two different tubs, you will want to think about how you will get the books to the tables during this transition to learn-about-the-world reading each day. You might just set the tubs on tables as you talk to them during this transition. You might have the kids do this job by designating someone from each table as the table leader. (This could be a rotating class job.) When you call for kids' attention at this transition point each day, you might ask your table leaders to switch the bins. This way only a few children are out of their seats, and it will make a smoother transition to this next kind of reading time each day.

Also, you might make these two charts back to back, perhaps by clipping them together. This way, each day when you switch from Old Favorite to learn-about-the-world reading, you can flip the chart to the side that will support their work. (This chart could flip just like the private/partner one.)

Readers Work Hard to Make the Words They Read Match the Page They Are Reading

IN THIS SESSION, you'll teach your readers the importance of reading the right part of their old favorite storybooks on the right page.

GETTING READY

✔ Put the gathering song words close by so that you can refer to it (see Connection). 👏

✔ Display the "We are Storybook Readers!" chart you started yesterday on the easel, with today's strategy—"Make the words and pictures match."—ready to be added (see Connection and Link). 👏

✔ Have a familiar emergent storybook you've read aloud several times ready to use. We suggest *The Three Billy Goats Gruff* (see Teaching)

✔ Have ready the Stages of Emergent Storybook Reading document to use during conferring (see Conferring and Small-Group Work) 👏

✔ You may choose to give each partnership a stuffed animal or an action figure to read to, to help them practice reading aloud in a clear voice (see Transition to Partner Time).

✔ Lots of nonfiction books in the table tubs (see Share)

MINILESSON

CONNECTION

Celebrate the strong work students did yesterday, and rally children to make the words they say match the words on the page.

We had settled on the rug, with the kids facing the lyrics of our gathering song. I began by reminding them of how amazing yesterday really was. For our first day with old favorite storybooks, I thought our workshop had been filled with smart readers doing smart reading.

"Readers, your first go at reading old favorite storybooks yesterday was terrific. On the way to school today, I was thinking about what I might teach you to help you make your reading *even better*. Then I remembered something I saw a lot of you doing yesterday. Do you want to hear what it was?"

Many kids nodded yes, and one of them was still slowly making his way to the minilesson. Waving him in, I continued.

"Here is what I saw. Lots of you got so into remembering the story as you read that you started to lose track of where you were in the book. The story sounded good, but it was a little confusing to listen to you read because the words did not always match the pictures. Then I remembered that that sometimes happens to us in another part of our day."

I pointed to the lyrics of our gathering song, hung on the wall, and said, "These are the words to our gathering song. Whenever we sing this, I point to the words so that kids can follow along and stay together. But sometimes we get so into the song that we stop paying attention to where we are on the page. When our singing does not match the page, we get confused and it's hard to stay together. It even gets hard to understand the words of the song!"

"We do sing like that sometimes," Kevin said.

"It sounds bad," Bryan added.

I answered, "As readers, we never want to get confused and not understand." Looking at the two boys, I added, "We never want to sound bad either." I smiled.

 Name the teaching point.

"Today I want to teach you that when you read an old favorite storybook—really, when you read *any*thing—you need to pay attention to what's on *that* page. You've gotta make *your* words match the *book's* picture and words. So, you need to study the page *carefully*."

I added to the chart:

Our use of the word *readers within this lesson and across the other lessons in this series is intentional. A huge part of your work in this unit is to convince your students that they are readers and to induct them into a broad literary tradition. By naming your students as readers, you help them begin to identify as readers themselves.*

```
┌─────────────────────────────────────────────────────┐
│ ┌──────────┐                                          │
│ │ ANCHOR   │     We Are Storybook Readers!            │
│ │ CHART    │                                          │
│ └──────────┘   • We look at the pictures, remember,   │
│                  read!                                 │
│                • We make the words and pictures match. │
└─────────────────────────────────────────────────────┘
```

We make the words
and the pictures
match.

TEACHING

Demonstrate reading words that do not match the page, and show how you catch your mistake by noticing that your words and the pictures do not match.

Turning past the beginning of *The Three Billy Goats Gruff*, I quickly reminded the class how the story started and then turned to page 9, where the troll first appears and is sitting under the bridge.

I said, "Watch me as I read the next few pages and as I check to see if my reading matches the page."

I began to read the page like my kids would—not reading conventionally. I made sure the children could see the pictures as I read. "On the way to the hill the goats had to go on a bridge and there was a troll under there who was mean. 'Who's that walking over my bridge?' And the little billy goat said . . .'"

I turned the page and showed students the picture of the youngest Billy Goat Gruff about to cross the bridge. With a confused look, I stared at the page. "Huh," I said to myself out loud.

To give my students a chance to engage in my demonstration, I prolonged my pause and I exaggerated my confusion at this mismatch of words and picture.

The kids were already up on their knees, eager to coach me. "Wait," I said to them. "This doesn't match. I already read about the little goat walking and the troll yelling. But, all of that troll yelling did not happen on the last page." I turned back to page 9, showing the troll under the bridge. "It happens on this *next* page, where the goat is walking over the bridge." I turned the page to show the youngest goat walking over the bridge, and I pointed to the picture. "I think I read this part of the story too soon."

I looked up at the class and asked, "Did you see me notice that my reading and the page did not match?"

The children replied with a chorus of yeses.

Show students how you fix your reading by returning to the last page where your reading matched the pictures and rereading to make the words and pictures match on every page.

"Now I have to do something to fix this up." I turned back to the page with the troll sitting under the bridge and said, "To fix up my reading when it does not match the page, I can always go back to the last page where it *did* match and reread to make it match again."

I did that, making my reading match the pictures on the page. "On the way to the hill, the goats had to go on a bridge. There was a troll living under there who was mean." I paused and dramatically turned the page.

This time I read making sure my reading matched the pictures. "First the youngest Billy Goat Gruff decided to cross the bridge. 'Trip, trap, trip, trap!' went the bridge. 'Who's that tripping over my bridge?' roared the Troll."

"It's fixed now," Anna said.

There were smiles all around.

ACTIVE ENGAGEMENT

Read on in the text, and recruit students to notice when you're reading doesn't match the page.

"Do you think you can help me in another place in the book?" I asked, and turned to page 13, showing the picture of the little goat and the troll talking.

"Listen to me read, and if you think I have stopped matching my words with what is actually on the page, will you stop me? Then, if we need to, we can work to fix up my reading."

I began to read, purposefully demonstrating reading ahead in the story without turning the page:

The work of making your reading match the pictures and the right part of the story is really all about monitoring your reading. Learning how to monitor or pay attention to your reading is perhaps the most important reading skill.

Sometimes evidence of monitoring is verbal and easy to see. It can sound like, "I get it," or "I don't get it." Sometimes monitoring is nonverbal—furrowed brows, pauses, or appeals to you can all be signs that a child has noticed something is wrong. It is important to remember that the noticing is always worth reinforcing even if it doesn't always lead to fixing.

"Oh, it's only I, the tiniest Billy Goat Gruff," said the Billy Goat in his very small voice.

"And I'm going to the meadow to make myself fat."

"No you're not," said the Troll, "for I'm coming to gobble you up!"

"Oh, please don't take me. I'm too little that I am," said the Billy Goat. "Wait till the second Billy Goat Gruff comes. He's much bigger."

The troll yelled, "Go away!" Then the next billy goat came and the troll yelled, "Who's that walking on my bridge?"

I turned the page and was deluged with cries of "It doesn't match!"

Rally students to reread the pages you just read with a partner, making sure their reading matches the pictures on the page.

Looking at the class, I said, "With your partner, fix these two pages up now so that they match. Go!" I listened in as kids reread the first page. I voiced over, "Don't forget to study the page carefully. What do you see happening in the picture? What do you remember happening in the story on this page?"

As their reading slowed to a stop, I turned to the next page and they read again. Before some of them could move on with the story and create another mismatch, I called them back together.

LINK

Encourage children to make sure their reading matches the page as they go off to read.

"Nice job, readers! It can be tricky to make your reading match the pages. But if you pay attention and use both what you can see in the pictures *and* what you remember about the story," I pointed to the chart as I said this, "you will be able to make everything match, and in the end, you will not get lost in your story. Matching helps you understand your old favorites.

"Remember that after you finish one book, you will want to move to another old favorite. You are going to want to take your time and make a masterpiece of your reading in each book.

"Off you go."

You will notice here that my approximated reading is pretty fancy. Sometimes I am trying to make my modeled reading more like kids' reading, such as when I want to help them make their current work better. Other times I make my reading more elaborate to give the kids a vision of what I hope they will be able to do more and more of as they keep reading their Old Favorite Storybooks.

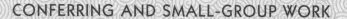

Making More Meaning from Books by Following the Actions Closely

AS CHILDREN READ THEIR OLD FAVORITES TODAY, some students may do very little reading per page. Elizabeth Sulzby would say that these children are in the first two stages of emergent storybook reading. They are either labeling and commenting on the pictures or they are labeling the actions to follow the story a little. These first two stages of emergent storybook reading belong to the same larger category of meaning making, which is reading that makes use of the pictures but does not yet include a formed story or story language.

For example, you might hear a child say about the first page, "There are three goats and they are all different sizes," or about the second page, "The goats are going up the hill to eat." Both of these readings match the pictures, but they do not yet hold together like a story. Your conferring and small-group work might aim to coach these kinds of readers to follow the actions in the story more closely so that they are grasping more of the parts.

As you work with children reading the second page, you might say, "Oh yeah, so this page goes kind of like this: 'The three billy goats went up the hill *because* they were hungry *and* they wanted to get something to eat up there. I remember . . .'" Then you could ask the kids to try reading it again themselves. Notice in this example that you add more of the action on the page but you don't name what you did. Instead, you use your voice to emphasize the additions you made.

Of course, your students will be at all different levels with this work. It's likely some students have reached the third and fourth stages of emergent storybook reading. Here, the story will be formed, but it will be read with the same everyday oral language kids use when they are on the playground. You might hear students say, "This is a story about three goats who have to cross over a bridge. The troll says, 'Who's going

over my bridge?'" or using a similar sequence but omitting the lines of dialogue, such as "There were three goats who had to cross a bridge, but a troll stopped them and asked where they were going." You might gather these students together for a small group and demonstrate for them how you read a page using story language. Opening up to the fourth page, you might say, "Let me read this page so it sounds like the book: 'It's just me, the littlest goat,' said the tiny goat. 'I'm going to the meadow.' 'No you're not!' the troll yelled. 'I'll gobble you up.'" Then, ask kids to practice reading the same page, and coach them as they try a few more pages.

To quickly determine where students fall, consider carrying the Stages of Emergent Storybook Reading document with you as you confer with readers. (This chart is available in the online resources, and a smaller verison is shown on the next page.) Observe as students read, notice what stage of emergent storybook reading they fall in, and plan your conferring and implicit modeling accordingly.

MID-WORKSHOP TEACHING
Celebrating Readers Who Self-Correct

"Readers, eyes up here. I'm seeing something that we've got to stop and celebrate. I actually saw *four* readers do what I did earlier that I thought only *college kids* could do on their own. This is it. These kids were reading along when they realized they had lost hold of the story. They were just saying stuff without actually matching it to the page. So you know what they did? They went back to the beginning and reread to make what they said match the page. This is something you can all do as you keep reading!"

"Today has been such an important day. Let's celebrate. Readers, seeing as how you have been doing college work—stopping when you need to and going back to reread and fix things up—I figure it's time for me to stop being the one who reads alouds to the kids, and it is time for *you* to do that. So I'm going to give each partnership a kid. (It won't be a real kid, but will you make believe it's real?)"

You might choose to give each partnership an action figure or a stuffed animal to read to. You will help ensure the work they do reading aloud feels authentic and important by giving your kids an audience (albeit a super quiet and passive audience) to read to.

I continued, "Will you work together and do a read-aloud of one of your old favorite storybooks? One of you hold the kid, and halfway be the kid. Look at the pictures, and listen carefully, and get excited like you do when I read to you. And will the other partner read aloud the start of the book? Then you can switch places."

The children were so excited that they almost started without my coaching. I tucked in a tip, anyway.

"Remember to read like me. Read to your 'kid' the way I do to you—with a big, clear voice. Check that your words match what's actually happening on the page, and point to the pictures to show that match."

Stages of Emergent Storybook Reading

Classification Scheme	An Example of a Child Reading	Conferring Suggestions
Category: Story not formed and reading governed by pictures *(Using meaning and syntax sources of information)*		
1. Labeling and commenting	"Look at that guy. He's got a lot of hats on his head . . ."	Add action and comments.
2. Labels with actions, which follow the action on the page.	"The guy is walking through the town . . ."	Add more action toward the big idea: What's that? What's happening?
Category: Story formed and reading governed by pictures and sounds like oral language *(Using meaning and syntax sources of information)*		
3. Dialogic storytelling—telling the story in dialogue using the pictures and oral language	"You see this is a story about a guy who sells hats for 50 cents. He says, 'Caps for sale! Caps for Sale!'"	Mimic the child's observations in the picture using dialogic storytelling and extend.
4. Monologic storytelling—telling the story in narrative sequence, not in dialogue, using the pictures and oral language.	A guy tries to sell hats. He does not sell any. He rests under a tree. Then monkeys steal his hats.	Comment on the picture using story or narrative language.
Category: Story formed and reading governed by pictures and sounds like story/written language *(Using meaning and syntax sources of information)*		
5. Reading using the pictures with a mix of oral storytelling and story language	"The guy walked for a long time. He said, 'I'm going to rest here.'"	Use story language as you add to what's happening.
6. Sounds like they are reading using story language without elaboration, but they are really using the picture	"He walked for a long time until he came to a tree. He sat down and leaned back . . ."	Begin to connect one page to another with expression—by linking one action to another with transition words.
Category: Story formed and reading governed by pictures and sounds like story/written language *(Using meaning and syntax sources of information)*		
7. Sounds like they are reading the story with elaboration, but they are really using the picture.	"He walked for a long time until he came to a tree (pause) a great big tree. 'That's a nice place for a rest,' thought he. And he sat down very slowly and leaned back against, leaned back little by little against the tree trunk . . ."	Be an active listener responding to what is happening in the story as they read: "Oh! Wow! Oh my, what's next?"

Transitioning to Learn-about-the-World Books

Channel children to choose a nonfiction book, share its topic with the class, and then read using what they learned about making sure the words and pictures match.

From the middle of the room I said, "We have ten more minutes for reading, and again, let's use that time for learn-about-the-world reading. I know you are dying for a chance to read about . . . what? Volcanoes? Yoyos? Horses? Right now, take a learn-about-the-world book from the table tub and get ready to call out what your topic is. What will the book teach you about?"

The children looked over their books for ten seconds and then I said, "On the count of three, get ready to shout your learn-about-the-world topic out loud to the world."

I counted and they shouted.

Quieting them, I said, "Here's one quick tip I have for when you read your learn-about-the-world books. You can use your old favorite storybook reading skills to help you read *any* book. That's it. You got it? Look at the page and say the words that are on that page. And what about if you get messed up? What do you (and college kids) do? You reread!"

During Bend I, your initial assessments revealed a diverse set of needs. Use the time you have while students are reading their learn-about-the-world books to confer with students one-on-one. Remember that you will want to move quickly from child to child and from table to table during this time. Your kindergarten children only need tiny bits of teaching at a time. Be careful not to plant yourself in one place, because you will not be giving enough kids attention and you may be giving the few you do see too much teaching.

Again, after about ten more minutes of reading, you will want to gather your children for a second read-aloud. A second read-aloud each day will help you add more old favorite titles to your table tubs. You will probably want to use the read-aloud plan for The Carrot Seed *to help you do a powerful read-aloud of any new titles.*

Session 12

Readers Know How to Get Their Own Old Favorite Storybooks

MINILESSON

In the connection, you will probably want to remind your readers of how well they are beginning to read their old favorite storybooks. You might also remind them how they seem to be falling in love with these books, too.

You might lead to your teaching point by saying something like "When you all were reading to your stuffed animals yesterday, I saw readers who were clearly in love with their books. You read them as if you wanted your stuffed animals to fall in love with them, too. Watching you made me think about how many more books should get so much love and attention, so they might become old favorite storybooks."

For the teaching point you might say, "Today I want to teach you how to make *new* old favorite storybooks. First, you find a storybook and a person you love. Then, you get that person to read the book again and again, while you listen closely. Then, you're ready to read it! This helps you have more books to fall in love with."

As you reference the steps, add them to the "How to Make an Old Favorite" chart.

How to Make an Old Favorite

1. Find a storybook and a person you love.

2. Ask, "Will you read this to me, please?"

3. Say, "Read it again," every time it is over.

4. Listen really closely.

5. **YOU** read it!

Teach children that many books can become old favorite storybooks, and highlight a few of the titles you gathered. Read the titles and give a quick commercial for a handful of the books, saving the rest of the title-giving and commercial-delivering for reading time.

Next, you could role-play how you use the steps above to turn one of the new books you highlighted into an old favorite storybook. Pretend your way through the steps, and refer to the chart as you do so.

During the active engagement, hand out books to partners and have them pretend to do the steps from the chart. Be prepared to give a tip or two as students work. For example, you could coach them to work on their convincing faces for steps 2 and 3. Or you might remind kids to use what they have learned so far in the unit when they get to the part where they read the book back to someone in step 5.

In your link, you might tell your class that for the first few minutes of private reading time, you want them to choose a new book to take home. Let them know you are hoping they'll read this book again and again at home and that it will soon reappear in the classroom as an old favorite storybook. Ask them first to take a book walk in their soon-to-be old favorite storybook so they can get to know it a little. And then remind them that they will move on to reading the old favorites that are already in the table tubs.

Every time you encourage your kids to have their own favorite books, you are helping them develop their identities as readers. Recruiting parental involvement in this process will make all the difference in the world.

As you know, we have been reading up a storm everyday during reading workshop. Our goal is to declare, in another few weeks that, "We are Readers!"

In order to reach our goal, we need you. The amount of time you spend reading to and with your children will make a huge difference to their growth in this unit and... forever. Reading together increases vocabulary, sparks conversation, leads to snuggling, uncovers new passions, leads you down paths with new friends and grows knowledge about the world. Reading is crucial and that is why we have a mission for you.

We are asking you to join us in an effort to reach our goal for this unit. This work is big and if we are going to do it we need all hands on deck. We hope you will join us.

Tonight your child will come home with a personally chosen book that he or she has a slight crush on and will come ask you to read it. When your child says, "Read it again," we would ask that you say, "Yes! With pleasure!" Your mission then is to help your child fall head over heels in love with this book by reading it over and over. Once your child has heard the story many times, we would love for you to invite him/her to read the book back to you.

Your child will not actually be able to read this book like you do, but we still call what they do reading. They will use what they remember and the pictures to read words to you. They will probably not look very much at the actual words in the book. Please do not think this work is about getting them to sound out words—these books are too complex for that yet.

You can make this your child's favorite part of the day by just being you. Don't worry about being a teacher here. Encourage the 'reading' of many words per page. Laugh at the funny parts. Ask questions when you have them for real. In the end, just follow your child's lead.

And, don't worry. We will be working toward really reading all year in kindergarten. We want you to know though that the work we are asking you to help with right now is the beginning of really reading and will set down a strong foundation upon which to build.

After your child has read the book to you many times, we are hoping that you will send this book back to school so that your child can share this reading with classmates. We hope this will happen by _____.

Thanks in advance for joining our mission. Your children will never be the same, in the best ways possible! Here's to all declaring together this year, "WE ARE **ALL** READERS!"

Warmly,

Your Kindergarten Teacher

FIG. 12–1   A letter to parents recruiting their support in making more Old Favorite Storybooks

CONFERRING AND SMALL-GROUP WORK

For your conferring and small-group work, support students by moving around the room and giving each child his own copy of the "How to Make an Old Favorite" chart. Once you've handed out the charts, build excitement for the books kids will be reading. Then have children place the chart in their potential old favorite storybook and put it in their backpacks so they remember to take it home.

Mid-Workshop Teaching

For your mid-workshop teaching point, be sure to transition your readers to some private reading time of their old favorite storybooks. Pull out the "We Are Storybook Readers!" chart to remind students of all the work they know how to do.

Transition to Partner Time

For your partner work, set students up to read old favorite storybooks together. Support partnerships as they work by noticing what they need, demonstrating a bit, and then encouraging students to try the work, just as you did yesterday.

SHARE

Today's share session can again be time for reading learn-about-the-world books. During these ten minutes, you will want to rely on your student observations to help you prompt kids to do all they already know how to do as readers of information books.

This lesson is extremely important because it helps make a home-school connection. You might also want to send a letter home to encourage families to read and reread the book that is coming home. You might make this an official homework assignment for the whole week. Your letter could also explain a little bit about how rereading books and then listening as kids approximate the reading of those books is an important first step toward conventional reading.

Readers Use Exact Character Words

IN THIS SESSION, you'll teach students that readers make their old favorite storybook readings better by using exact character words.

📌

GETTING READY

✔ *The Three Billy Goats Gruff, The Carrot Seed,* or another familiar emergent storybook (see Connection and Teaching and Active Engagement)

✔ Display the "We Are Storybook Readers!" chart on the easel and have ready the new strategy Post-it—"We talk like the characters." (which looks like a speech bubble coming from a character's mouth) (see Link).

✔ Conferring sheet (see Conferring and Small-Group Work)

✔ Have the "Readers Read with a Partner" chart readily accessible (see Transition to Partner Time).

✔ Make some or have the kids make (at another time—perhaps during choice time) troll stick puppets and goats stick puppets. (see Teaching, Active Engagement, and Link).

✔ Before you begin your minilesson, you could highlight children who have turned books into old favorites and then point out how you have new books in your old favorites collection.

MINILESSON

CONNECTION

Read aloud, supporting children to impersonate the characters and say their words, then celebrate the way they brought those characters to life, becoming them.

"Let's start with some reading," I said, and began rereading *The Three Billy Goats Gruff*. I worked hard to invite my kindergarten students to join in, especially to the reading of the dialogue. After a few pages of yelling like trolls and persuading like goats ("My brother is coming soon. He is much juicier!") I closed the book.

I began, "You know what? You know that book so well. You are starting to turn into the characters!" I leaned into this idea a little more by saying, "Like Yamilah. You were the littlest billy goat on this page when you said, 'Oh, it's only I, the tiniest Billy Goat Gruff.' Those were that little billy goat's exact words. **You** were **him!**"

Yamilah laughed a little.

And Joey, "You *were* the troll on this page when you said, 'Well then, be off with you!' When you said that, Joey, I could have sworn that the troll was right here on the rug with us!" Then with a tiny pause and big eyes, I added, "During *read-aloud*. A troll.

"Our read-aloud was better because of all of your troll words and your goat words."

❖ **Name the teaching point.**

"Today I want to teach you that when you are reading your old favorite storybooks aloud (or even if it is just to yourself) you can make the story sound really great by putting in the *exact words* the characters say. The exact words make the characters come to life. Those characters come right into our reading workshop."

TEACHING

Demonstrate reading a section of an old favorite storybook. Show students how you make a predictable mistake—summarizing instead of using exact dialogue—and recruit them to assess your work.

I turned to the page of *The Three Billy Goats Gruff* where the troll is telling the littlest billy goat to get off his bridge. "Readers, do you remember this part of the story? Look at the picture. Thumbs up if you got it. Okay, now let me try reading it, and you check me to see if I am using the exact words of the characters."

Demonstrating what *not to* do, I summarized: "The troll told the goat that he was going to eat him up." Then I stopped and checked in with the kids, asking, "How was that? Were those words exactly what the troll said?" I knew the answer was no way. Some kids seemed unsure.

I demonstrated again, this time summarizing the goat's dialogue. "The goat told the troll to wait for his brother." Again I shifted out of reenacting to debrief with the kids. "How was that? Were *those* the *exact* same words the goat said?" More kids seemed sure my words didn't match the goat's words.

Introduce puppets depicting characters from your old favorite read-aloud and use them to show students how to do this work, quoting the characters.

"We really want these characters to live here with us in our workshop." I revealed two stick puppets—a troll and a goat. The kids oohed and aahed. "If we want these characters to live here, we need to make these puppets talk. He needs to say his true words. Let me try again, and this time, I will try to say the exact words."

Again I held up the troll puppet, but this time I spoke in a troll voice. I said, "No, you're not, . . . for I'm coming to gobble you up!'" And with the goat puppet and in a goat voice, I said, "'Oh, please don't take me. I'm too little, that I am,' said the Billy Goat. "Wait till the second Billy Goat Gruff comes. He's much bigger."

"Good," Lydia coached, and other kids nodded along.

Resting the puppets on my lap, I said, "That was better right? I made my characters talk in that part and on that page of the story by saying their exact words."

ACTIVE ENGAGEMENT

Direct children to try saying the characters' exact words on the same page, talking as if they were the puppets.

"Now it is your turn. On this same page, I want you all to make the troll and the goat talk. I just did it, but now it is your turn. With your rug partner right now, decide who will be the troll and who will be the goat."

Here you are demonstrating for students what not to do by summarizing a character's dialogue instead of using the character's exact words. Demonstrating this makes it more likely that students will catch themselves, or their partners, slipping into summary, and that they will be reminded to say a character's exact words.

FIG. 13–1   Puppets used to practice reading exact character dialogue

****

I paused a few seconds for the decision.

"Okay, goats, raise your hands. Trolls, raise your hands."

"Okay, when I hold up the puppet, you talk like that character. Here we go," and I held up the troll. I listened in as kids tried their parts. Before I switched to the goat puppet I said, "Do not forget to say what the character says. When you do that, you will probably use the words *I* and *me* and *you*."

I then held up the goat puppet and the kids tried again.

I called them back together after a few more seconds and said, "We are going to try the last part of the page together. After the goat says, 'Do not eat me, wait for my middle brother,' do you remember what happens? The troll tells him to go away. Let's try to talk like the troll in this part now."

I held up the troll puppet once more. All together we said our versions of *go away*. Most of those versions sounded nothing like the actual words from the book, but most of the versions did sound like the character talking.

LINK

Remind children that they will not have puppets as they read privately, but that they can touch the characters on the page and use their fingers to help.

As the *Go away nows* and the *Get off my bridges* died down, I said, "Readers, really amazing old favorite reading has character's exact words in it. We learned today that it can sometimes be tricky to get the words just right. Our puppets helped us realize that when the character takes the stage, he just needs to talk."

I added the strategy to our "We Are Storybook Readers!" anchor chart.

Worrying that kids might think they needed puppets for every time they read an old favorite, I continued, "So today, when you go off to read your old favorite storybooks, you will not have puppets, but you could use your fingers to help." I touched the troll and said his words. "See what I did? Instead of making a puppet talk, I touched the character and made him talk right on the page. Watch again."

I touched the goat and he said his words. "Did you see that? Touch the character and make him talk. You all can do this in every old favorite you have."

Know that not every partnership will have figured this out neatly and that some partnerships will both be goats and some will both be trolls. Doing the task perfectly does not matter as much as getting some practice with the dialogue skill right now.

We talk like the characters.

If your kids are very tied to the puppets, you might put puppet-making materials such as construction paper and Popsicle sticks in an art center so that kids can make their own puppets during choice time. (In most kindergartens, there are thirty to forty-five minutes set aside each day for kids to have free choice time to work/play at the project of their choosing.)

Supporting Student Development over Time

As YOUR STUDENTS ARE READING THEIR OLD FAVORITE STORYBOOKS, you will want to think about reading with them and next to them just like a parent or other loved one might. You will also want to think about helping your readers get better and better at reading these rich stories. Many of us have found it helpful to think about watching our children develop in a more focused way. In other words, if you are using Sulzby's stages of development to monitor progress in your students' reading,

MID WORKSHOP TEACHING
Reading Lines of Dialogue with Feeling

I sang our attention-getting song and then said, "Readers, you were so good at reading 'Who's that tripping over my bridge?' like you really knew what that troll was feeling. But when I listen to you read at your tables, some of the time you are reading the words that characters say in a *blah* way. So I have a tip for you."

I made quick eye contact with all of the parts of the room. "When you are getting ready to say the words of a character, and you put your finger on the page to help you do that, make sure you take an extra second to notice the character's feeling in that part of the story and on that page. Like before you say the little goat's words, 'Please don't take me. I am too little. Wait till the second Billy Goat Gruff comes. He's much bigger,' take a second and notice how he is feeling right there in that part.

"To me, the littlest goat looks like he is nervous and scared in this part. Someone *huge* is trying to eat him!" I then said the dialogue twice. Once without feeling and once with feeling. "So as you read, notice how the character is feeling, and then read the words they say with the feeling they are feeling."

TRANSITION TO PARTNER TIME   Rally Partners to Pause and Think about What They Are Reading

"Readers, you have been doing such an amazing job reading your old favorites together during partner time. I am watching you taking turns on pages or trying to read with your voices together on every page. Your reading is sounding better and better. Can you feel it?"

I waited for them to react.

"I just wanted to teach you that even as you are practicing *reading* your old favorites, I also wanted to remind you to *talk* about them, too. On each page, after you read it, you might also pause before turning the page and try to say what you are thinking on that page. You might do this thinking about the book by starting off with, 'I think . . .' Remember, you guys, that we added a pinch of ourselves to our learn-about-the-world books by making sure to say *I think*, too!"

then you might be sure to observe them reading the *same* book each time you come to them.

For instance, you might listen in to a child as he reads a few pages of *The Carrot Seed*. You will want to transcribe what his reading sounds like to help you classify his stage of development. Remember that your transcription does not have to be for the whole book. A couple pages of careful listening and transcribing will help you record data that will help you monitor for growth. You could then plan to listen in as he reads that *same* book again a few more times during the unit. By focusing in on one book, you will be better able to look for signs that his emergent storybook reading is getting

(continues)

better and better. Of course, he will be reading other old favorites during the unit, but you will be tracking his growth in just one book. Once you get to know a child's strengths in one book, it should make it easier to prompt the child to transfer what he has learned to other books.

If you decide to work in this way, your notes will probably look something like what you see here. (A blank Emergent Reading Conferring Sheet is available in the online resources.)

Also, it is very important that you flit, butterfly-style, from child to child with only a quick stop for coaching. You will want to listen in to and give light, quick feedback to something like half your class (not a quarter or less) each day as they read during reading workshop. To move with this kind of pace, it can help to have a schedule of who you need to see each day. Without a schedule, your kindergarten students will very likely succeed at pulling you away from supporting everyone and into supporting just a few of them. (After all, they actually *all* need you *all* of the time.)

Once you have arrived at a child who you need to see, you will want to already be thinking about how you will leave. A timer can help you make sure you are spending two or three minutes per child. Be ready to listen in and take notes for thirty seconds to a minute and then read with the child for another minute to lift the level of what she can do. And then, be ready to move on!

Emergent Reading Conferring Sheet

Name _____

Old Favorite Title _____

Date _____
Read #1

Date _____
Read #2

Date _____
Read #3

Transitioning to Learn-about-the-World Reading

Remind students that they can learn more from their learn-about-the-world books by using their finger to study all parts of each page.

"Readers, eyes here please. As you switch from old favorites to learn-about-the-world books, I want you to remember that you can learn so much more while you are reading these books if you use your finger to touch parts of the page and read what you see there. There may not be characters talking in these books, but you can still use your finger to make sure that you are looking closely at all the parts of the page as you are reading."

As the kids reached for our beautiful information books, I added, "I am setting our timer for ten more minutes. I want to challenge you to learn as much as you can about the whole wide world before time runs out. Ready? Read!"

As your workshop ends today, you will probably be ready to begin another interactive writing book. If you have written a third of your class into the first book, "Things Our Class Likes to Do," then you can write the next third of your class into a new book. Perhaps you will write "Things Our Class Likes to Eat." This book could have pages that are patterned and use high-frequency words. This new book might read, "Aiden and Riley like to eat pizza. Yamilah and Sammy like to eat noodles . . ." Remember that you will want to make time for kids to add illustrations to these books so that when you read them later there will be picture support for their reading.

Readers Reread Old Favorites, Remembering to Say More and More of the Story

IN THIS SESSION, you'll teach your students how to use the words on the page to push themselves to say more when reading their old favorite storybooks.

GETTING READY

✔ Have a familiar emergent storybook ready. This should be a Big Book or a text you can place under the document camera. We suggest *The Three Billy Goats Gruff* (see Teaching and Active Engagement).

✔ Prepare a familiar song to sing with students as they transition to the rug. We suggest a song that supports students in hearing sounds in the beginning of words (see Connection).

✔ Before you begin your minilesson, you could continue to highlight children who have turned books into old favorites and then point out how we have new books in our old favorite collection.

✔ Display the "We are Storybook Readers!" chart on the easel (see Active Engagement). 👏

✔ Choose a familiar informational text—we use *The Beetle Alphabet Book*—to demonstrate how students can now read more words (see Share).

✔ Review kids' reading choices and be prepared to refer to one that has the word *and* in the title during the share.

✔ Display a chart that shows a familiar word students have learned to read. We recommend a chart that shows the alphabet song (see Share).

MINILESSON

CONNECTION

Sing your class a (phonemic awareness) song to provide practice in hearing sounds in the beginning of words.

To the tune of "Old MacDonald," I sang my class to the rug. We had been learning letters and the sounds those letters make during name study and word work in these first days of school. I used this song to practice hearing sounds in the beginning of words, and I often did this as part of our transitions from one part of the day to the next. I sang:

> What is the sound that starts these words—
> Fit and frog and fun,
> /F/ is the sound that starts these words—
> Fit and frog and fun.
>
> With a /f/, /f/ here
> And a /f/, /f/ there
> Here a /f/, there a /f/
> Everywhere a /f/, /f/.
>
> /F/ is the sound that starts these words—
> Fit and frog and fun.

Remind students of the work they did including character voices in their old favorite storybook readings.

As the song ended, I began, "Yesterday we read in the voices of the characters in our books. It was so fun to watch you all talk like the characters in your books. It was like the characters had come to life in our room. We had goats and trolls and dads and boys."

Kevin said, "And there was Max and Ruby here too from my book."

Smiling, I continued, "You all are sounding more and more like the books every day. And I noticed that just a few of you are starting to do something that the rest of you have probably not noticed. I think this is a thing you could all do. Today I want to help you know one more thing that will help you make your reading of old favorites sound more like how grown-ups read them."

❧ **Name the teaching point.**

"Today I want to teach you that sometimes when you go back to *reread* a storybook, you remember *more* of the story, and that means you can say more on each page. And if there are a lot of words on the page, then there's a lot of story to tell."

TEACHING

Explain that when readers reread a text, they sometimes get stuck, repeating the same words they said before without making them better.

"I want to show you what I do when I am reading, and especially when I am rereading these old favorites." I opened up to the second page of *The Three Billy Goats Gruff*. "Once you have read a book many times, it can sometimes happen that you get stuck on each page. But this kind of stuck is different. Because you have heard the book so many times, you *don't* get stuck when it comes to what to say on the page. Instead, you tend to get stuck on how to *make better* what you say on the page."

There were a few creased eyebrows, so I began my demonstration.

"Watch. I have read this page many times. It goes, 'There were three billy goats who were hungry and they were all called Gruff.'

"Because I have read this page many times, this could be how I read this page every time I read it from now on. But if I am going to get *better* at reading this story, I need to not get stuck reading the book the same way each time."

So far we have taught kids several strategies to help them read more on each page. In this session, we are trying to turn our kids toward the words in their books. While we definitely don't expect kids to completely read these books conventionally yet, we do want them to know that the written words control how we read the story. This look-to-the-word-quantity strategy can also help kids self-prompt for elaboration on a page.

Demonstrate how noticing the general number of words helps you decide how much to read on a page.

"One thing I do is I study the pictures and characters and remember the story to help me read the page. Then, before I turn the page, I take a quick glance down to the words. I am not really reading all of those words. I am really just noticing how *many* there are. If there are a lot of words, I try to say a lot of words when I read."

"You could say more words on that page, we think," Dylan said, and he pointed to the book.

"Okay. Let me try this page again." This time I said, "'There were three billy goats and they were hungry and they were called Gruff,' but I do see more words there, so I am going to try to read more on this page."

I ran my finger around the page and thought out loud. "I remember this part. They wanted to go up the hill to get grass and some kind of flower, and they wanted to eat and eat to get fat. Yeah! That's how this page goes."

Read all of the words together so that the kids can hear how much better the second try got.

"Listen to this page now you guys. 'There were three billy goats and they were called Gruff. They were hungry and they wanted to go up the hill to get grass and flowers. They wanted to eat and eat and get fat.'"

Nodding my head and trying to look extra proud at my efforts, I said, "Now this part is better. This page now has more words that tell more about what is happening in this part of the story."

ACTIVE ENGAGEMENT

Encourage students to read a new page, noticing how many words are on the page and making their reading match the general number of words they see.

"Now it's your turn," I said as I turned to the page where the littlest billy goat was facing the troll on the bridge. "Let's first think together for a second about how to read this page."

Lilly called, "The littlest billy goat said it was only him and he wanted to cross the bridge, and the troll said, 'No, I'm going to eat you instead.'"

"Okay. Let's check the picture and the story. Does what Lilly read match what is happening in that part?"

After many nods from the class, Luke said again, "But look at all those words over there."

"Yes. There are a lot of words. Right now, when I say, 'Go,' I want you to turn to your partner and try to add to what Lilly read on this page by remembering this part of the story and by looking carefully at this page. Go."

Voices trickled at first and then built to a bit of a rush as the kids worked together to figure out this page.

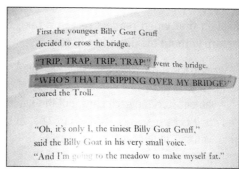

FIG. 14–1 Pages with different amounts of text

After I listened in to several partnerships, I could hear that most of them had remembered the goat's response to the troll on this page, so I decided to read it all together.

"Readers, we saw all of those words on this page, and most of you read something like, 'The littlest billy goat said it was just him and he was going to make himself fat. And the troll said'—join in everyone—'No, you're not! I'm coming to gobble you up.'" Most kids joined in.

"Then, a lot of you added something about how the littlest goat answered. You read something like, 'No, don't take me because I'm too little. Wait for the second billy goat!'"

Debrief. Name the important work the readers just did.

Smiling and nodding a bit, as if I was impressed by our better reading, I gestured toward our "We Are Storybook Readers!" chart, and I touched each strategy as I talked. "We read by remembering this part of the story and by studying the page and by thinking about the character's words. Then, we added even more because we saw more words. Now this page sounds more like the way a grown-up would read it."

LINK

Send children off to read, reminding them to study the words to be sure they are saying as much as the author wrote.

"As you head off to read your own books today, I want to remind you that when you reread your old favorites, you are trying to make them better each time. Your job as you keep reading these same titles is not to read them the exact same way each time. Your job is to read them in a better way each time.

"Today we realized that one way to make your rereading better is by glancing over at the words and trying to see if what you read seems to be as much as the author wrote on the page. If there are more words *written*, then you can try to *say* more words when you read.

"I can't wait to watch your book reading get so, so much better today. Off you go!"

Moving Kids toward More Sophisticated Reading of an Old Favorite Storybook

I PULLED UP NEXT TO AIDEN AND TOOK A SEAT. Even though he was a few pages into *Caps for Sale*, I asked him to turn back to the beginning of the book so I could listen to him from the start. As he turned to the front, I looked over my notes. I had listened to him read this book once before. I had noted that he used the pictures and his understanding of the story to read the book with a mixture of his own language and a tiny bit of book language.

Aiden began to read. "Once upon a time, there was a man that sold hats. He carried them on his head. He said, 'Caps! Caps for sale! Fifty cents a cap!'"

Based on my previous observation and after hearing him read just this little bit, I made a quick decision to teach into the actual language of the book.

"Aiden, listen to how this page goes."

I read, "Once there was a *peddler* who sold caps. He carried them on *top of* his head." As I read, I pointed to the pictures to help emphasize the italic book words from the line above.

I then read the part of the page he forgot. I said, "Then it goes, 'First he had his own checked cap, then a bunch of gray caps, brown caps, blue caps, and red caps on the very top.'" Again, I pointed to the stack of caps as I read this part.

Aiden nodded his head, and I asked, "What do you think will happen next?"

"No one wants to buy the caps," he answered.

I read the next page and then asked Aiden to read the first *two* pages back to me again. This time the man was a peddler and he remembered to stack the caps. Aiden also read most of the second page almost exactly right. I wrote in my notes "Caps for Sale, p.1/p.2 strong book language." I also wrote, "connecting words" to help me remember next steps because this skill was still tricky for him.

Because my goal was to spend no more than three minutes with Aiden, so that I would be able to move on to many more children during this workshop, I decided to pause his reading and leave him with a tiny tip. I said, "I love how you are trying to read the exact words of this book. Keep doing that."

I headed off to a child that, according to my notes, I had not read with in a while.

MID-WORKSHOP TEACHING
Matching Reading with the Amount of Text on the Page

"Readers, I love the way you are checking the words and pushing to say more when there are lots of words. Sometimes, it can feel like you have read everything on the page, but if right before you turn the page, you quickly check where the words are, you might see that there is more to read. Try that quick check before you turn the page right now. Read the page. Then, right before you turn the page, quickly check to see if what you read matched how much was on the page."

TRANSITION TO PARTNER TIME   Make Sure the Amount Partners Read Matches How Much Text Is on the Page

"Partners, when you read your old favorites today make sure that together you are looking at where the words are and trying to match your reading to the words. If there are a lot of words, then you should try to say a lot of words. If the words are broken into groups on the page, then try to help each other remember what all of the different parts were about to help you read more of each page."

Transitioning to Learn-about-the-World Books

Highlight examples of words students can read now that they could not read before, and tell the story of how they read each word.

As the students put their old favorites back into the baskets and grabbed high-interest learn-about-the-world books, I reminded them, "You have read so many of these books so many times already, and you have also learned so many things about letters in kindergarten so far. Because of your reading and your letter learning, I know that when you go back to the words, *after* figuring out what the page teaches from the pictures and other cool features, I know that you will see more in the words. I want you to try this in your learn-about-the-world books today."

I held up our beetle book. "See this book? We read this book a bunch of times in the very first days of kindergarten, but we could not read these words. We thought this book was called *The Beetle Book* because of the picture on the cover, but then once we got inside the book, we realized this was a letter book, too. We went back to the title and saw the word that started with the letter *a*. Because the letter *a* goes /a/, we figured out that this extra word was *alphabet*. We then read the *a* word in the title. *Alphabet* worked because it starts with the /a/ sound and it is a letter book. Remember that?"

After the kids smiled, I finished, "It happened again yesterday. When Michael was rereading the title and the cover of his book," I held it up, "he saw this word," and I pointed under *and*. "Michael came running up to me and said, 'I found *and*.' You remember when we saw that word in our alphabet song?"

I pointed to our alphabet song chart (written with line breaks that would make it easier to sing with one-to-one match) and underlined the <u>and</u>.

a b	j k	t u v
c d	l m n o p	w x
e f g	q r s	y and z
h i		

Challenge readers to read more and more words on each page.

"Readers, don't forget to look at the words, too, in your learn-about-the-world books today. You have learned so much already about letters and words that you can bring to your books as you reread them!"

As this workshop ends, you may want to do another read-aloud to introduce a new old favorite storybook read-aloud title to the tubs for kids to read. Remember that within the next few sessions, you will want to have about five titles in your old favorite tubs.

During word study time each day, you may be doing two different kinds of work to help your kids learn letters and sounds. You might be doing Patricia Cunningham's star name work, and you might be doing explicit teaching of letters and sounds.

Readers Use Special Connecting Words to Put Storybook Pages Together

IN THIS SESSION, you'll teach your kids to use words to connect one page to the next page to make their old favorite storybooks sound better.

GETTING READY

✔ You will need the piece of writing you have been using as your teacher demonstration piece for writing workshop. The pages of your story should be unstapled and written across three pages of writing paper (see Connection, Teaching, and Link).

✔ You will need your demonstration text that you have been using in the previous lessons. We suggest *The Three Billy Goats Gruff* (see Teaching and Active Engagement).

✔ Get your "We Are Storybook Readers!" chart out, and be ready to add the strategy "We use words to join the pages together" (see Link and Transition to Partner Time).

✔ Stages of Emergent Storybook Reading document (see Conferring and Small-Group Work)

✔ Make sure you have your copy of *The Beetle Alphabet Book* (see Share).

MINILESSON

CONNECTION

Read aloud your story from writing workshop, placing extra emphasis on transitional words and phrases.

As my kindergartners gathered on the rug, I turned toward a piece of my writing that I had been using to teach during writing workshop. I had each page hung separately, side by side on the easel. It was a simple story with extremely detailed drawings of me playing on the swings at the playground, and it was drawn across three pages that were unstapled. There were no sentences—just labels.

"Do you all remember this story from the last few days? This is my swing story that I wrote during writing workshop. Let me read it to you so that you remember it." As I touched the pictures with my finger and paused a little, remembering parts, I read page 1 by using the pictures to remember how the story went (remember that there are no written sentences in my story, yet).

"*On a windy day*, I sat down on the swing. It was a little tight on me. I pushed myself just a little with my toe at first. The swing moved a tiny bit. It was hard."

Turning to page 2 I read, "*Then* I moved my legs in and out. The swing started to go a little more." I moved my finger and touched each character as I said their dialogue. "My mom asked, 'Do you want a push?' I said, 'No thanks. I can do it myself.'"

And finally on page 3, I read, "*After a long time*, I went high in the sky. I looked at the clouds and I felt like I was as high as the trees. My mom was smiling at me." I pointed to my smiling face in the picture as I read this last part. "I was happy."

Connect the work you did as a writer to the work students are doing reading their old favorite storybooks.

After some timid applause, I continued, "This is my story from writing workshop, but it reminded me of the old favorite storybooks you all have been *reading* during reading workshop. My story has pictures that help me remember parts of the story and that help me remember the words to read on each page. Your old favorites have those things too. My story has characters talking, and your old favorites do too.

"But there is one big thing that I have been noticing when you all read your old favorites that you do not have, that my story does have. My story, from writing workshop, uses words to help connect the pages of my book. Listen and watch."

Reread your story, highlighting the transitional words and phrases. Explain that these words connect the pages of your story, and staple the pages into one booklet to help illustrate the cohesion.

I reread the story and I stressed the connecting words. When I said, "On a windy day," I took page one off the easel and held it in my hand. As I read, "Then," I took the second page off the easel and slipped it behind page 1. I then read, "After a long time," and slid page 3 behind the first two pages.

"Did you see and hear that, readers? I use words to connect my pages. They work almost like a staple does to hold my pages together." I restacked the pages as I said, "On a windy day," "Then," and "After a long time." "These words connect my pages together." I stapled all three together.

"Connecting words turn these pages of my writing into a story that makes better sense because with those words we know how all of the parts go together."

❖ **Name the teaching point.**

"Today I want to teach you that one way to make your reading of old favorite storybooks sound more grown-up is to read the words that make the pages go together. You read one page and then put in connecting words like *and then* . . . and *after that* . . . and then you read the next page."

TEACHING

Read your demonstration text, and think aloud about what transition words you could use to connect the pages. Tuck in tips as you demonstrate.

I picked up *Three Billy Goats Gruff* and continued. "You just watched me use special words to help me put my pages together in my writing. Now I want you to watch me put my pages together in my *reading*."

I turned a little further ahead in the book to the part where the littlest goat first sees the troll. After reminding the class of how we got to this part in the story, I said, "I can read this page by using pictures and the story and the character's talking and a glance at the words.

On a windy day

Then

After a long time

FIG. 15–1   A 3-page teacher story to teach connecting words.

"This page goes, 'First the youngest Billy Goat Gruff decided to cross the bridge. "Trip, trap, trip, trap!" went the bridge. "Who's that tripping over my bridge?" roared the Troll." You see, I just read this page. Now it is time to turn the page. As I turn the page, watch me try to say my connecting words."

I read again the last little bit of the current page, "'Who's that tripping over my bridge?'" and then I turned the page slowly as I looked forward to the next page. "Readers, putting in these connecting words can be tricky when you have only read a book a few times, but now, we have read this book so many times. When I turn the page, as the page is falling, I can look to the page that is coming to help me make some connecting words."

I repeated, "'Who's that tripping over my bridge?'" and then said, "I remember the part that is coming. I can see the picture that is coming to help me remember. The goat whispers back at the troll. Now I have to think about what words go between 'Who's that tripping over my bridge?' and "Oh, it's only I, the tiniest Billy Goat Gruff," said the Billy Goat in his very small voice.'"

I continued to think aloud. "I could just say *then* or *and* as I turn the page. *Then* and *and* make good connecting words. Listen to see if my pages sound connected now." I reread the pages. "'Who's that tripping over my bridge?' *Then* the little goat whispered, 'Oh, it's only I, the tiniest Billy Goat Gruff . . . And I'm going to the meadow to make myself fat.'"

I looked up from the book. "How did that sound? Did you hear my special connecting word?"

"Then," Bryan called.

"Did you see how I thought about the connecting word I might say as I turned from one page to another?"

ACTIVE ENGAGEMENT

Recruit students to generate connecting words for the next few pages of the text.

"It's your turn. Let's do another page together. Okay? This page continues, 'No you're not,' said the Troll, 'for I'm coming to gobble you up!' 'Oh, please don't take me. I'm too little, that I am,' said the Billy Goat. 'Wait till the second Billy Goat Gruff comes. He's much bigger.' 'Well then, be off with you,' said the Troll." Now we are going to turn the page and think about saying a connecting word."

I lifted the page slowly and coached. "Remember the goat begging and the troll sending him away. Now what do we say to get to the next page? Here comes the medium-size goat. You remember this part. What connecting words could we say?"

Joey said, "A few minutes later. Say, 'A few minutes later.' It works."

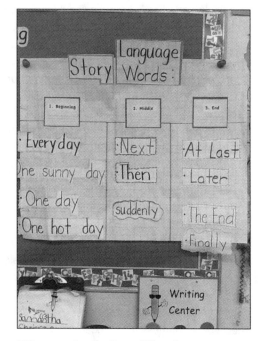

FIG. 15–2   A collection of Story Language Words

I said, "Let's all try it. Let's start from what the troll says." I touched the troll on the page and we all said, "'Well then, be off with you,' said the Troll." I turned the page super slowly, and the kids joined me in saying, "After a few minutes."

As the page fell, we finished reading that part, "A little later the second Billy Goat Gruff came to cross the bridge . . . 'Who's that tripping over my bridge?' roared the Troll." It was beautiful.

We continued the process for another page, choosing the connecting word *and* to join the troll's yelling with the middle goat's response.

LINK

Remind children to use glue words as they read, and add the new skill to your chart.

Holding my stapled story up next to our *Billy Goats Gruff* book, I said, "You are all really getting it. In both writing and reading, stories make so much more sense if we try to connect the pages with words. As we are turning the page, we can look back and look forward to try to think of words that join those two parts together." As I said this, I joined my two hands together to symbolize connecting pages.

I pointed to our chart. "I added this to our chart. I wrote, 'We use words to join our pages together.' This is one more thing that old favorite storybook readers do. We used *then* and *a few minutes later* and *and* to help us in our goat storybook. I used *then* and *after a long time* in my swing story. I can't wait to hear the words **you** use as you turn the pages of your old favorites today!"

ANCHOR CHART

We Are Storybook Readers!

- We look at the pictures, remember, read!
- We make the words and pictures match.
- We talk like the characters.
- **We use words to join the pages together.**

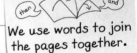

We use words to join the pages together.

Supporting Readers in Linking Pages of Text

A S YOUR READERS HEAD OFF eagerly to try to do all they have already learned to make the reading of their old favorite storybooks even better, you will want to notice how students are using connecting words in all of the different books they are reading. Today, you'll ask students to practice this work across their private reading, partner reading, and learn-about-the-world book reading. It's likely you'll be highlighting these words as authors use them in your read-alouds also, putting extra emphasis on the words that your favorite authors use to glue pages of their texts together.

The work of accumulating text and linking pages together sounds sophisticated. However, in practice within this emergent storybook work it sounds more like, "The

third Billy Goat Gruff went 'Trip! Trap! Trip! Trap!' across the bridge, and the bridge went 'Creak!' 'cause he was so heavy, *and right away* the troll screamed, 'Who's that trip trapping over my bridge?' *and then* the third billy goat yelled loud, 'It is me.'"

(continues)

MID-WORKSHOP TEACHING
Using Time Words to Help Connect the Pages

"Readers, eyes here please. I see so many of you trying to use connecting words when you are turning pages. I just want to share a tip with you to help you find the right words. As you turn the page, you want to think about time. It is kind of like you need a *when* word, a time word as you turn the page. So, as you turn the page, you could ask yourself, 'When?' Very often, your answer to this question will help you connect the pages."

I held them a few seconds longer to elaborate.

I used a familiar example to demonstrate this work. "Remember when the troll said, 'Go away!' and the next page has the middle billy goat coming? If, as I turn the page, I ask, 'When?' then my answer might be 'a few minutes later.' Hey, that was cool! We said 'a few minutes later' when we connected the pages earlier. You see that? Asking and then answering 'When?' works."

TRANSITION TO PARTNER TIME
Readers the Full Repertoire of Their Storybook Reading Work

"Hey, readers, during partner time today, I have a mission for you. You are going to be reading your books together as usual. And I thought today it might be fun for you to concentrate a little extra on putting all the work you've learned to do as storybook readers together. Right now, will you help me read through our 'We Are Storybook Readers!' chart? Let's remember all the work that we can do as we read our old favorite storybooks." I read through our anchor chart, inviting students to chime in and read with me.

ANCHOR CHART

We Are Storybook Readers!

- We look at the pictures, remember, read!
- We make the words and pictures match.
- We talk like the characters.
- We use words to join the pages together.

"You've got important work to do today, readers. I will be around to admire your grown-up-sounding reading."

You'll see students who are grasping this work use transition words to connect pages to one another by linking actions and events from one page to the next. This is the work you'll support when students are in Elizabeth's Sulzby's sixth level of emergent storybook reading.

As you support students with this work, remember Sulzby's research about the benefits of implicit teaching. Your conversations with readers might sound more like a parent talking about a book than a teacher. When a child finishes reading a page, you might say, "I don't get that. . . . These pages go together?" As you ask this, model turning the page back to revisit the page you just read. Very early on, we want our readers to know that readers do the work of understanding a story both by turning back and turning ahead or feeding back and feeding forward.

Additionally, you might support this work by asking students to predict what will happen next in the text. It may seem unnecessary to ask readers to predict in books they've read many times before. However, by asking students to predict, you are really building important habits and behaviors in your early readers. Here, prediction is not really about getting it right or wrong. Instead, prediction is used as a way to get a running start at the next page. It also helps students to connect the events on one page to what is happening on the subsequent page. Once you notice children reading pages with elaboration and remembering most of the parts by using the pictures, you could ask, "What do you think will happen next?"

Of course, you will probably also want to continue to monitor progress in your readers by transcribing bits of their reading, returning to the same text so you can track growth over time. A page or two of reading is all you need before you can switch to offering coaching and support. As you transcribe, remember that your goal is to collect more little bits of data, not to record perfect data once or twice across the whole bend.

Stages of Emergent Storybook Reading

Classification Scheme	An Example of a Child Reading	Conferring Suggestions
Category: Story not formed and reading governed by pictures *(Using meaning and syntax sources of information)*		
1. Labeling and commenting	"Look at that guy. He's got a lot of hats on his head . . ."	Add action and comments.
2. Labels with actions, which follow the action on the page.	"The guy is walking through the town . . ."	Add more action toward the big idea: What's that? What's happening?
Category: Story formed and reading governed by pictures and sounds like oral language *(Using meaning and syntax sources of information)*		
3. Dialogic storytelling—telling the story in dialogue using the pictures and oral language	"You see this is a story about a guy who sells hats for 50 cents. He says, 'Caps for sale! Caps for Sale!'"	Mimic the child's observations in the picture using dialogic storytelling and extend.
4. Monologic storytelling—telling the story in narrative sequence, not in dialogue, using the pictures and oral language.	A guy tries to sell hats. He does not sell any. He rests under a tree. Then monkeys steal his hats.	Comment on the picture using story or narrative language.
Category: Story formed and reading governed by pictures and sounds like story/written language *(Using meaning and syntax sources of information)*		
5. Reading using the pictures with a mix of oral storytelling and story language	"The guy walked for a long time. He said, 'I'm going to rest here.'"	Use story language as you add to what's happening.
6. Sounds like they are reading using story language without elaboration, but they are really using the picture	"He walked for a long time until he came to a tree. He sat down and leaned back . . ."	Begin to connect one page to another with expression—by linking one action to another with transition words.
Category: Story formed and reading governed by pictures and sounds like story/written language *(Using meaning and syntax sources of information)*		
7. Sounds like they are reading the story with elaboration, but they are really using the picture.	"He walked for a long time until he came to a tree (pause) a great big tree. 'That's a nice place for a rest,' thought he. And he sat down very slowly and leaned back against, leaned back little by little against the tree trunk . . ."	Be an active listener responding to what is happening in the story as they read: "Oh! Wow! Oh my, what's next?"

Transitioning to Learn-about-the-World Reading

Prompt readers to read words that help pages go together.

"It is time for learn-about-the-world reading. I am wondering if you can work to try to connect the pages together in these books, too. As you turn the page in your book that teaches about a topic, you will want to try to see if you can say some words that help the pages go together.

"Probably all of the pages go together in one way because they all teach about the same thing, the same topic. Maybe the pages of *The Beetle Alphabet Book* connect like 'A is for African Goliath Beetle, B is for Bombardier Beetle.'"

At the end of this workshop, you will want to do another read-aloud of an old favorite storybook. You will probably want to reread the new title that you started during your last session. Keep in mind that each title needs to be scaffolded by reading them aloud at least three to five times before you give that book to kids to read on their own.

Again, this is more about habit than getting it exactly right. We are trying to get kindergarten readers to engage in important behaviors right from the beginning of their reading. Knowing that all of the pages go together and then trying to put the pages together are important reading understandings and behaviors.

Readers Use More and More Words that Are Exactly the Same in Their Old Favorites

MINILESSON

IN THIS SESSION, you'll teach your students that the more times they read a book, the more they will sound exactly like the book.

CONNECTION

Play a familiar song and explain to the children that knowing all the words to a song they love is just like knowing the words to a familiar book.

Just before the kids were all completely settled on the rug, I began in earnest. "You are really becoming expert old favorite storybook readers! Right now, for just a few seconds would you look up here?" And I pointed to the easel, where I had displayed several of our old favorites. I paused so the kids could really look.

"These are our old favorites. Right now, would you decide which of these books you read the best, and would you tell your partner about reading that book? Ready? Pick one. And . . . go!"

After the kids talked about their reading and their books for about a minute, I said, "You were talking about your books and I was thinking about how *well* you are beginning to read them. That's what happens when you read a book again and again. In some ways, these books are like the songs we sing again and again too!"

I reached over and pressed Play on a popular song that I had cued up to the chorus.

As the music registered with my kindergartners, I said, "This is a song that you have heard again and again," and before I finished my last word, all voices were singing along.

As the chorus ended, I paused the song and continued. "You see, you have heard that song again and again. This part of the song is the part that repeats over and over, and you've heard it so many times you even know the exact words that are in this part. You all knew the words *so* well, that you almost sounded like the singer of the song."

GETTING READY

✔ Find a popular song that the children have heard again and again. Cue up this song to the chorus, so that you are ready to press Play at a part that the children will recognize (see Connection).

✔ Choose an old favorite storybook that you have used throughout the unit. We suggest *The Carrot Seed* (see Teaching).

✔ Prepare a second old favorite that you have used in previous lessons. We suggest *The Three Billy Goats Gruff* (see Active Engagement).

✔ Have the "We Are Storybook Readers!" chart handy and be ready to add a new strategy Post-it—"We read more and more exact words." (see Link).

✔ Stages of Emergent Storybook Reading document (see Conferring and Small-Group Work)

I gestured back to our old favorites collection.

"Sounding just like the book and knowing the exact words in a song reminds me of what is beginning to happen in your old favorite storybooks."

❧ Name the teaching point.

"Today I want to teach you that when you read a book over and over again you try to use some of the exact words from the book. Some of the words, especially words that repeat, become words that you know by heart. They become words that you can say exactly like the book says them."

TEACHING

Demonstrate reading a familiar text with incorrect wording, and recruit children to correct your reading based on their knowledge of how the text goes.

Grabbing *The Carrot Seed* from the easel, I continued. "We have read this book again and again. You are doing such amazing reading in this book. You are using the pictures and thinking about the story, and you are making the characters talk. You are even trying to use words to connect the pages."

I opened the book. "Because you are doing such good reading, it can sometimes be tricky to figure out ways to keep making your reading even better. But when you read a book again and again, you start to be able to read the exact words in the book, especially the words that repeat."

I began to flip through the pages a little and said, "Watch me do this exact word reading, even just a little bit, in *The Carrot Seed*." I began to read, making sure that my reading looked like and sounded like my students' reading. In other words, my reading was not correct, but it was close to the text. It definitely made sense, and it sounded like my version of the author's words.

"Once upon a time, a little boy planted a seed and wished it would grow. His mom said," and I paused, modeling thinking by placing the book in my lap for a second. I said, "I know she does not think that the seed will grow. Okay, I know how this page goes."

Pulling the book up from my lap, I resumed reading. "Mom said, 'It is not going to grow.'"

As I went to turn the page, a bunch of my kindergarteners were shaking their heads.

"What?" I fake-asked to their disagreement, and I continued on to the next page

"The dad said, 'It isn't going to grow.'"

This lesson has music incorporated into it. Music is probably a huge part of the rest of the day too. You can sing all of the old favorite songs with your kids: The Itsy Bitsy Spider, Hickory Dickory Dock, and Twinkle, Twinkle will all grow your kids as readers. They will also be fun! Fun matters because how your learners feel about something effects how well they learn it.

This time kids were yelling, "Nooooo."

Aiden said, "Ms. Louis, we know what the parents say. They say, 'I'm afraid it won't come up.'"

I nodded my head. "You're right! This part happens a few times in the book and that *is* how the book talks. So, especially in the parts that repeat, I can try to read the exact words in that part."

I turned back two pages and asked the kids to join me in reading the exact words.

Debrief. Name the work you just did for students.

"Did you see how to make my reading even better, I thought about parts of the book that repeated, and I tried to read those parts using the exact words from the book? Those are words I know by heart, so I can read them every time I read this book."

ACTIVE ENGAGEMENT

Encourage children to read a second old favorite with you, chiming in on the words they know by heart.

As we finished our "I'm afraid it won't come ups," I said, "Hey, I wonder if we could do this exact word reading in any other part of another one of our old favorites?"

I picked up *The Three Billy Goats Gruff*. "There are repeating parts in this book. Like when each goat comes on the bridge they make the same sound when they walk. That's one thing that repeats. What else in this book repeats? Turn and remember with your partner."

After I heard the children talk about how the goats answer the troll the same way and how what the troll says back repeats, I asked them to join me in reading the exact words in those parts.

We read the parts where the goats walked across the bridge. "Trip, trap. Trip, trap," and I said, "Yes! Exact words."

We roared, "Who's that tripping over my bridge?" I said, "Exact words."

And, we pleaded, "Oh please don't take me." And again, I answered, "Exact words," giving kids a big thumbs up.

FIG. 16–1 The highlighted portions show examples of some kinds of language that is easy for beginning readers to read exactly.

LINK

Motivate children to go off and read their texts with more and more exact words of the book.

"Readers, as you head off to read, I want you to remember that we now have *one more way* to make our reading of our old favorites even better. I want you to remember that the words that repeat in a story are like the parts of songs that repeat. In the parts where the words repeat, you can say the *exact* words. You can talk *exactly* like the book." I added the new strategy to our growing chart.

> ### ANCHOR CHART
>
> ### We Are Storybook Readers!
>
> - We look at the pictures, remember, read!
> - We make the words and pictures match.
> - We talk like the characters.
> - We use words to join the pages together.
> - **We read more and more exact words.**

I took a breath and asked, "Who feels ready to think about parts that repeat and try to be exact-word-readers in those parts?"

Many kids raised their hands and Sammy said, "It will be so cool!"

And I, unable to resist, answered, "Exactly!"

Investing in Language and Early Reading Behaviors

AS YOUR KIDS HEAD OFF TO READ, you may be feeling a little torn. Sometimes, as this unit moves on, you might begin to have doubts that this work, this nonconventional reading work, will pay off. You may have heard people talking about how you need to get your kindergartners into leveled books. Or you may have had parents tell you, "They are just memorizing the books," and ask, "When will they start their *real* reading work?" Parents may say, "They are just looking at the pictures." They may ask if they should cover the pictures so the words will be looked at instead. Urge them *not* to cover the illustrations.

So, right about now, even as you can see that your kids can do so much more in their books, you may be having doubts. But remember, language is the basis of all literacy learning. This investment in language and early reading behaviors will pay off in huge ways in the end. Keep in mind that the next unit in kindergarten will invite children to read more and more conventionally. So if you have children who you think might be ready for leveled books, the next unit is the place to do that work. If, however, you are worrying that you have kids who could benefit from more sessions of old favorite storybook reading, refer to the *If . . . Then . . .* book.

(continues)

MID-WORKSHOP TEACHING
Focusing on the Easier to Exact-Read Parts of Books

"Readers, find me please." I stood closest to my most unfocused readers, and I even put my hand on the shoulder of one.

"I just wanted to give you a little tip as you read your old favorites today. I just wanted to let you know that there are specific places in your book that are easier to get the exact words for. We already know that parts that repeat are easier to read exactly right. But you can often read the very beginning exactly right if you listen closely, and the ending too. Also, it can be easy to read exactly what characters say in different parts of the story."

I held up four fingers and touched each one as I quick-listed easier to exact-read parts of books. I said, "So now you know that repeating parts, beginnings and endings, and character talk are parts that are easier to get exactly right. Back to your reading. Try to focus on the parts that are easier to read exactly right."

TRANSITION TO PARTNER TIME   Modelling Rereading and Talking about an Old Favorite to Get It Exactly Right

"Readers, as you sit hip-to-hip today with your book in the middle between partners, I want you to try to concentrate on getting some parts of your books *exactly* right. One way you can do this is by rereading some of the key parts of your books. Listen carefully to each other and try the part more than one time to see if you can get it more and more exactly correct."

Holding *The Three Billy Goats Gruff*, I said, "Watch me try this rereading. 'There were three Billy Goats Gruff and they wanted to go up the hill.' That's good, but I remembered, because we have read this story so many times, that there is more in this part."

I looked out at the class. "Let me try this part again. 'There once were three billy goats and their name was Gruff. They wanted to go up the hill to eat daisies and to get fat.' Did I get more exact words, readers?" They nodded enthusiastically. "Yes. That is more like it. Today you will want to use rereading of keys parts to make your old favorite readings better and better. Readers, also don't forget to talk about what you are thinking as you read through your storybooks."

Until then, you will want to continue using the Sulzby emergent storybook stages to look at your kids as readers. By the end of this unit, your goal is to get many kids to stage 7 (or higher).

At this stage, children are using the illustrations and the structure of the story and a lot of the actual language of the book to read their old favorites. They may not yet be noticing the words or be beginning to point to them as they read, but that becomes bigger work in the next unit. As you ask students to read you a chunk of a familiar old favorite storybook, be on the lookout for your kids' reading of these books to begin to sound more and more like how you would read these books. Likely, there will be times when, if you close your eyes, you hear children reading whole chunks of the books that sound exactly or almost exactly the same as your reading.

Offer students who are at stage 7 in their old favorite storybook reading additional support. Likely, these are the students who are beginning to attend more to the words in their books. To support them in beginning to read words, you might provide them with easier emergent storybooks, reading these books aloud several times until they become old favorites. You have already turned *The Carrot Seed* into an old favorite. Other storybooks that might be easier to read conventionally include *Where the Wild Things Are*, *Knufflebunny*, or *The Very Hungry Caterpillar*. These books feature less text per page, making it much easier for readers to access the words on the page. However, they still contain strong picture support, a clear story structure, and rich language.

As students read these books, you will want to encourage them to begin pointing under words. This will not be a one-to-one match kind of reading. Rather, when kids first begin to point to words in their old favorites, they'll be pointing after they read, not using pointing to help them read. You can continue to use these easier emergent storybooks in your next unit to support students who need additional time to grow their language. This work will be particularly beneficial for readers who have not yet gotten to stage 7.

Remember, also, that there is certainly a place for repeated readings of more complex books. The richer story language and the more complex story structure of harder emergent storybooks will continue to be instrumental in growing your readers, whether they are very close to conventional reading or not quite yet.

Stages of Emergent Storybook Reading

Classification Scheme	An Example of a Child Reading	Conferring Suggestions
Category: Story not formed and reading governed by pictures *(Using meaning and syntax sources of information)*		
1. Labeling and commenting	"Look at that guy. He's got a lot of hats on his head . . ."	Add action and comments.
2. Labels with actions, which follow the action on the page.	"The guy is walking through the town . . ."	Add more action toward the big idea: What's that? What's happening?
Category: Story formed and reading governed by pictures and sounds like oral language *(Using meaning and syntax sources of information)*		
3. Dialogic storytelling—telling the story in dialogue using the pictures and oral language	"You see this is a story about a guy who sells hats for 50 cents. He says, 'Caps for sale! Caps for Sale!'"	Mimic the child's observations in the picture using dialogic storytelling and extend.
4. Monologic storytelling—telling the story in narrative sequence, not in dialogue, using the pictures and oral language.	A guy tries to sell hats. He does not sell any. He rests under a tree. Then monkeys steal his hats.	Comment on the picture using story or narrative language.
Category: Story formed and reading governed by pictures and sounds like story/written language *(Using meaning and syntax sources of information)*		
5. Reading using the pictures with a mix of oral storytelling and story language	"The guy walked for a long time. He said, 'I'm going to rest here.'"	Use story language as you add to what's happening.
6. Sounds like they are reading using story language without elaboration, but they are really using the picture	"He walked for a long time until he came to a tree. He sat down and leaned back . . ."	Begin to connect one page to another with expression—by linking one action to another with transition words.
Category: Story formed and reading governed by pictures and sounds like story/written language *(Using meaning and syntax sources of information)*		
7. Sounds like they are reading the story with elaboration, but they are really using the picture.	"He walked for a long time until he came to a tree (pause) a great big tree. 'That's a nice place for a rest,' thought he. And he sat down very slowly and leaned back against, leaned back little by little against the tree trunk . . ."	Be an active listener responding to what is happening in the story as they read: "Oh! Wow! Oh my, what's next?"

Transitioning to Learn-about-the-World Reading

Rally children to reread so they can make their reading even better.

"Readers, I loved the rereading work you did in your old favorites today. As you switch to your learn-about-the-world reading, I want you to remember to keep rereading. Don't just let your partner or even yourself read and then quick, turn the page. Try that page once and then try it again. Try to make your second reading of a page even better than the first read.

"Now that you have been in kindergarten for many days, you know way more about how books and letters work. Try bringing your new smarts to your learn-about-the-world books.

"Maybe you read a book about sharks before and you only said a few words on each page. Use the photographs and imagine them moving to help you say more.

"Maybe you read a book about plants before and tried to read words but could not. Use your new letter/sound knowledge to hunt for words that you can read now."

Holding up some of our learn-about-the-world titles, I ended by saying, "In these books, rereading more exactly will help you get more exact learning."

As this reading workshop comes to an end, you might find yourself doing a shared reading. Because you are working each day during word study to teach your kids the letter names, formation, and sounds, you will want to get them using their increasing knowledge as they read books with you during shared reading. Remember that the next session in this unit and the next unit in your kindergarten year are both about beginning to put together all of the sources of information (meaning, syntax, and visual) to make meaning in books.

Readers Can Point to and Read Some Words in Their Old Favorites

IN THIS SESSION, you'll teach your kids how to use their know-it-by-heart power to help them point to and read some of the words in their books.

GETTING READY

✔ Bring one of your stories from writing workshop. This should be a three-page true story about your kindergarten self (see Connection).

✔ You will need a familiar old favorite storybook. We suggest *The Carrot Seed* (see Teaching).

✔ Choose a second familiar old favorite storybook. We suggest *The Three Billy Goats Gruff* (see Active Engagement).

✔ You will need a pointer to gesture under the first letters of words (see Teaching and Active Engagement).

✔ "We Are Storybook Readers!" anchor chart with new strategy Post-it—"We find, point to, and read some of the words." (see Link)

MINILESSON

CONNECTION

Reread one of your stories from writing workshop.

My kids settled into their rug spots. On the easel I had one of my true stories from writing workshop.

Ruby said, "I thought it was *reading* time."

Smiling, I said, "It is. But I put up a piece of my writing because yesterday when you were reading your old favorite storybooks, I saw *some* of you doing something that I wanted to teach to *all* of you. I thought I could teach that *reading* thing using *writing* first because I think you are *already* doing this thing in writing."

First, I reread a three-page, true story about my kindergarten self.

Make the connection between children reading the words of their own stories and reading the words in their old favorite storybooks.

I tapped the first page of my booklet and said, "My writing looks so much like your writing. We all have stories with meaningful pictures that we can read with beautiful story words. Thumbs up if your writing has those things—story and meaningful pictures and beautiful story words."

I continued. "I know. But, readers, you know what else your writing has? It has *words*. You have been working hard trying to use what you know about letters and sounds to put *words* in your writing too. And not only have you been working hard to *write* those words in your stories, but you have also been working hard to *read* those words too."

I pointed under some of the labels and invited the kids to read them with me.

"You can write and read words in your writing, and so I think you are ready to do a little of this reading work in your old favorite storybooks too."

❖ **Name the teaching point.**

"Today I want to teach you that when you read a book really well, you remember some of the exact words. Then, you can find those words and point to and read some of them—just like you do in writing workshop."

TEACHING

Demonstrate how you read the title of a book, pointing to each word you read. Then, show students how you notice the first letter in the words in the title.

I took down my writing and placed *The Carrot Seed* on the easel. "Readers, you are reading your old favorites more and more like I would read them. Each day, every time you practice, those books sound better and better. Finding and pointing to and reading some of the words in our books feels like the next thing we can do to take our old favorite reading to the next level."

Ramon interrupted. "I can already find and read some of the words in that book up there," and he got up, and before I could stop him he took our shared reading pointer from the easel ledge. "This says *The Carrot Seed*." (He read the title with one-to-one match for two of the three words.)

Reclaiming the pointer and reseating Ramon, I continued. "Ramon did read some of the words on the cover because he knows the title of this book. So it feels like the title of an old favorite could be the first place where we might be able to find and point to and read some of the words of a book. But I want to get you to do something extra once you read those words."

I placed my pointer under the words of the title. "Watch me. So, I know this book is called *The Carrot Seed*. And I can point to each word as I read what I already know. But I do one more thing. As I point, I make myself notice the letters in the words that I just read."

I moved my pointer back to the first word of the title. "This word starts with a *t*, and this next word is *carrot*, and it starts with a *c* because c-c-c-carrot, and *c* goes c-c-c. And, this last word is *seed*—sssssseed. *S* goes /s/. Did you see how I made myself notice the letters in the words from the title? The title can be very helpful when it comes to finding and pointing to and reading words in the other pages of your old favorites because usually those words show up some in the rest of the book."

I chose to read aloud a story that had very detailed pictures and included a lot of initial sound labels, as well as some final sound labels, on each page. If your class is writing sentences, then your writing piece might also include a sentence. However, for this lesson, I wanted the emphasis to be on the labels, since label reading more closely matches the kind of reading students will be introduced to in this lesson.

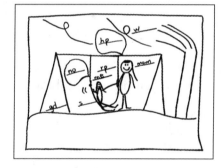

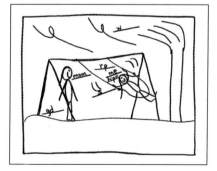

FIG. 17–1   The teacher's 3-page teacher story with labels added

Encourage students to help you find and read those familiar words in the first several pages of an old favorite, using the first letters.

I turned to the first page and said, "Now that I have paid extra attention to the words of the title, I can carry those words into the book. Now as I read this page, 'There once was a little boy who planted a carrot seed,' I can do one more thing. I can look to see if I know any words on this page."

Eva sang out, "I see *carrot*—that *c* word."

I pointed to it as several voices yelled about the *s* word being *seed*. Again I pointed to it and nodded at their reading.

ACTIVE ENGAGEMENT

Recruit partners to find familiar words on the cover of a different old favorite storybook and read them.

"Readers, let's try our word reading in another book." I pulled out *The Three Billy Goats Gruff*.

"When I say, 'Go,' I want you to turn knee to knee, eye to eye and point at the words that you know on the cover. Go."

As I moved around the rug, I was ready to listen for kids who were unable to read the title. I had my prompt for this ready. "Don't forget that you know this book really well. You know what the title is. Some of you are saying, 'I don't know what all those different words are on the cover.' But you do because you know the name of the book, the title."

Coach partners to notice the first letters in the words they just read. Then, invite them to read the first page in the book with you, first reading it like a story and then reading some words.

When Jamie and Tonya air-pointed and read the title correctly, I prompted to them and everyone else, "Don't forget to notice the letters in the words of the title—especially the first letters. Noticing letters can help you carry those words into the book with you as you try to find and point to and read more in your old favorites."

I turned to the first page of *The Three Billy Goats Gruff*. "Okay, ready. Eyes up for a minute. Stay knee to knee." I paused for eyes.

"Now let's see if we can both story-read this page and then find, point to, and read some words on this page too! First, remember and read this page with your partner and then try to use the title words to help read words on this page. Go."

Choruses of "Once upon a time" rang out as students first read the page as storytellers. Then, they shifted their attention to reading specific words. Predictably, some kids were saying again that they could not read all of the words on the page. I coached into the work of the whole class. "Remember that you are probably not going to be able to read all of those words yet. There are a lot of them. But, you know *some* of the words from the title. See if you can find them on the first page. What letters did they have in the beginning of them?"

Remember that a major focus of this unit is on helping children develop their own identities as readers, seeing themselves as people who can read. Your coaching here will reinforce this.

LINK

Send children off to read, and remind them that, now that they know their books by heart, they can begin to read some of the words.

Pulling the kids back together, I got ready to send them to their reading. "I saw so many of you find and point to and read 'The Three Billy Goats' on this page. I want you to continue to do the kind of reading you have been doing all along with these books."

I referred to our anchor chart and reminded them of all of the bullet points except the last one. I wanted my kindergartners to know that their main reading work was *not* reading the words.

ANCHOR CHART

We Are Storybook Readers!

- We look at the pictures, remember, read!
- We make the words and pictures match.
- We talk like the characters.
- We use words to join the pages together.
- We read more and more exact words.
- **We find, point to, and read some of the words.**

We find, point to, and read some of the words.

When I got to our new bullet, I said, "Word reading is just one more thing that you can add to your rereading of old favorites, and it really makes sense because you have begun to know these books by heart. Remember that you will often be able to read the title of your books and then use some of those title words as you try to read words in the pages of your storybooks."

Focusing on Word Reading and Meaning Making

THE WORK OF TODAY'S SESSION may feel too advanced for some of your kids. We first want to caution you to go easy with word reading. This is *not* a session on one-to-one matching. The purpose of this session is to encourage kids to do more in their old favorite storybooks. We *do* want kids to know that the words are important when reading a book. However, we are always trying to balance this emphasis on word reading with an emphasis on meaning making. If kids *can already* read words in these old favorites, we certainly do not want them to hold back because they hear us saying you do not need to read words to read these books. In other words, we never want our teaching to inadvertently encourage kids to do *less* than they are capable of doing.

Remember, though, that if you want kids to begin to get obsessed with letters and words, the first best place to do that is in writing workshop. First, because writing is the slowest literacy process, slower than reading, speaking, and listening, it allows for careful attention. Second, because writing ideas are generated from the personal experience and knowledge of the child, they can bring high levels of understanding to the creation of their texts. And third, writing is also highly motivating because kids are making things—books—about themselves.

For all three of these reasons, writing is often the place to work harder on words and letters. To make the best use of writing as a support for reading, you might follow some of the suggestions given on the next page.

- To encourage attention to letters, you should be sure to teach into letter formation. You will want to make sure that when teaching letter formation

(continues)

MID-WORKSHOP TEACHING   Finding Readable Words

"Readers, just look up for a minute please. I am listening to and watching you read. Some of you are realizing that it is easier to read words in the parts of your books that you can read exactly right."

I held up the mom page in *The Carrot Seed*. "Like on this page. Because we know that this page says, 'His mother said, "I'm afraid it won't come up,"' some kids could find the word *mother*, mmmmm-mother."

I pointed to the word *mother*. "That's the word with the letter *m*, that goes /m/ in the beginning. So remember that the parts where you are starting to know the exact words of your old favorites are also great places to look for words to point to and read. Remember, yesterday we said that maybe those words will be in repeating parts *or* when characters talk. Maybe readable words will be in the beginning or the ending of books too."

TRANSITION TO PARTNER TIME   Rallying Readers To Teach Their Partners Words They Can Read

As my kids got ready to read their old favorite storybooks with their partners, I called out a little tip to help focus their work.

"Today when you are reading together, you have an extra bit of exciting work to do. Today when you are reading together you can be doing all of your great old favorite storybook reading *and* you can be finding and pointing to some specific words."

I searched their eyes and said, "Cool. Right?! Each of you has read different words in your books during private reading time. Now, during partner time, you have the chance to teach each other the words that you read in your book."

---

you use verbal pathways, providing students with directions for how letters are made. There are many different handwriting programs, and each one has its own way of describing letter formation. What matters most is that you have consistency in the making of those letters.

- Use whole-class interactive writing to begin to make books for the next unit. You might take songs that the class knows—such as "Twinkle, Twinkle" or "The Itsy Bitsy Spider"—and then write them across pages during interactive writing. You will not be able to write these books in one day. But if the kids share the pen with you to make these texts, not only will they be engaged in using letters and sounds to make words, but they will also be better able to read those texts semiconventionally in the next unit.

- You will also want to be sure to get kids to reread their writing often. Be sure that you get them to read both the pictures using story structure and beautiful language *and* have them read their words by finding and pointing to them, in labels and in sentences.

Transitioning to Learn-about-the-World Reading

Review the steps for reading words work.

"You will switch to your books that teach you about so many different things in the world. I can't wait to admire the ways you find and read some specific words in those books too."

"Ms. Louis, I finally got the gross eating book [*Time to Eat*]—the one you read to us the other day," Anna said.

With a thumbs up, I continued, "Be sure to do the reading words work in the same way we did earlier in our learn-about-the-world books. First, remember what the page teaches and think about the words that the page probably uses to do that teaching. Then, search for a word or two by listening to one of the words you came up with, hearing a sound in the start of that word, and then thinking about the letter that makes that sound.

"The title can often help you get started with some word reading in a book. So it can pay off for you to try to figure out the title, and if you do not know the title of your book, you could just come ask me."

As this reading workshop ends, you might think about which balanced literacy component makes the most sense for your class. You might choose to do shared reading if you are seeing many children in your class who are beginning to read more conventionally. And if you have more kids that still have not started to sound a lot like the old favorite storybooks when they read them, then you may use a read-aloud to read again one of the newer titles in your table tubs.

You might also start another interactive writing book. Perhaps you will do this interactive writing each day after your morning meeting for about fifteen minutes. Maybe this book could be called Things Our Class Likes to Play. *Again, a third of your class could be in this book. Maybe the book reads, "Joey and Riley like to play Pokemon. Lola and Luke like to play soccer," and so on.*

Session 18

Readers Work with Their Partners, Using All They Know, to Read Old Favorites

MINILESSON

CONNECTION

Invite children to brainstorm why they think they have reading partners.

As the kids got themselves to the rug and as the final lines of "We Are Gathering" were sung, I looked in awe at our old favorite storybook reading chart.

IN THIS SESSION, you'll teach your kindergarten students to use the anchor chart for the unit as a checklist to help make their partner reading of their old favorite storybooks even better.

GETTING READY

✓ You will need the "We Are Storybook Readers!" chart (see Connection).

✓ Have the "Readers Read with a Partner" chart ready for use (see Teaching).

✓ Choose a familiar old favorite storybook that your students know by heart. We suggest *The Three Billy Goats Gruff* (see Teaching).

✓ Prepare a pile of old favorite storybooks to distribute to partnerships (see Active Engagement).

✓ Create a mini-chart titled "Powerful Partners Work as a Team!" with three bullet points (see Link).

✓ Display the "Readers LEARN from Books, Too!" chart from Bend I (see Share).

"Readers, we have learned to do *so* much in these first weeks of kindergarten. We have most definitely become great readers of old favorite storybooks."

I paused.

"We are also becoming great reading partners. But I started to wonder why you think we even *have* reading partners. So, when I say, 'Go,' I want you to turn and tell the person next to you why having a reading partner is good. You will probably start by saying, 'Having a reading partner is good because . . .' Go."

For thirty seconds I listened to kids say things like "We can do it together" and "It makes reading more fun."

I refocused the class by highlighting what a few readers shared. "You already know so much about why we have reading partners. I heard you say that partners let you do reading together and it makes it more fun. Those are probably just about the *best* reasons to have a reading partner. There is one more reason to have a partner that we have not talked about before."

❖ **Name the teaching point.**

"Today I want to teach you that powerful partners work as a team to try to wow their listeners. You can use the anchor charts from the unit as you work to make your old favorite storybook reading the best that it can be."

TEACHING

Recruit children to act as your reading partners, and rally them to read the "Readers Read with a Partner" chart with you.

"I want you to watch how I work with a partner to make my reading better. I want us all to be partners to practice this. So will all of you be my partner?" They all cheered, "Yes!" and I said, "If I could, I would squeeze all of you in this chair here so we could be hip to hip with the book in the middle."

After much giggling, I said, "The chair thing is not going to work, but we can *pretend* that we are hip to hip and book in the middle just for now, I think." They nodded.

"Okay. So we are going to work as partners to make our old favorite reading even better. First, I want us to remember what *better* means. Our chart can help us with that."

I invited the kids to read the "Readers Read with a Partner" chart with me, shared-reading style.

Charts will play an important role in this session and in your teaching all year long. Charts can help gather up your teaching and help kids track what they have been learning. A good chart can serve as another teacher in the room and help kids be more independent. When your kids can't remember what they should do next, looking at the chart can prompt them for your desired behaviors. Charts can also serve as shared reading texts for your kindergarten class. And the process of making a clear chart can help you understand your teaching better.

Decide how to read your old favorite storybook, in this case choosing see-saw reading. Invite students to see-saw read as your partner, alternating pages with you.

"First, we will reread the chart to remember what good storybook readers do. Then we will decide how we will read and then read."

After rereading the chart, I looked out at my "partners" and said, "I'm thinking we should see-saw read. See-saw reading gives us the chance to be both the reader and the listener in our partnership. We need both, but we especially need listeners so we can try to wow them!

"Now we choose see-saw reading and *read*. And, reading is, of course, the most important part. Will you read with me a little right now? Let's take turns. I'll go first, and when I am reading, you listen closely. I will do the same when you read. Try to make it your best by doing *everything* we know about reading old favorites well."

Demonstrate a low-level reading of the text, and recruit students to critique your reading and offer feedback.

Grabbing *The Three Billy Goats Gruff*, I decided to read the text in an intentionally weak way, by summarizing instead of storytelling and by not including any exact words from the text. I opened to the first page and read, "There were three goats and they were sitting in the grass."

I looked out at my partners for feedback. "How was that?"

Several kids told me my reading was fine, so I looked for the disapproving partner in the crowd.

I saw Matthew shaking his head no, so I gestured to him to share. "The first page don't go exactly like that, Ms. Louis."

"It doesn't?" I asked, feigning surprise.

"No. It doesn't, 'cause you had no exact words," he corrected. "It goes, 'Once upon a time, there were three Billy Goats Gruff and they wanted to go up the hill to eat flowers and make themselves fat.'"

Debrief. Name the work your partner just did to help you.

I said, "Readers, we just did step three! After I read a little bit of the book, just a page, I paused. And all of you, my partners, helped me check my reading using our chart to help you remember what to check for."

ACTIVE ENGAGEMENT

Direct children to strengthen their old favorite storybook reading by rereading the anchor chart, see-saw reading, and stopping regularly to check their reading.

"Will you try this again, but with a partner? When I say, 'Go,' I want you to turn knee to knee and say, 'Hello, partner,' and I will give you a book to share. Go."

I quickly handed one old favorite to each partnership. "Okay. Now will you fix your bodies so that you are ready to be reading partners?" The kids turned hip to hip and put the book across their laps. I reached out and corrected one partnership.

"Now you are ready to be partners who make your old favorites even better. Get started." Then I guided their practice as they worked by calling out the steps over the rug.

"First, remember what we have been learning by looking at our charts." I knelt down and invited two partnerships who needed support to read the chart with me shared-reading style. As my stronger readers began their books, I called, "Remember to see-saw read and listen to each other carefully." That coaching helped most other kids get started.

Within a few seconds, I voiced over, "Remember to stop and check your reading every page or two."

*Kindergarten students are still developing their oral language. When Matthew said, "The first page **don't** go exactly like that," notice how I just asked, "It **doesn't**?" I did not talk about his mistake. I just said it correctly and then Matthew said it back correctly. We always also have language goals for kindergarten kids, in addition to their reading and writing goals.*

You'll want to move students through these steps quickly, not letting them read more than a page or two before you stop them and remind them to check their reading. As you name the steps, listen to partner conversations for any signs that the children understand what it means to check their reading. You might hear students stop their partners and say, "No, that wasn't right!" or take over the page and read it more powerfully.

LINK

Remind readers of the powerful partner work they can do together, and send them off to read.

"Let me stop you, partners. I saw you all doing such amazing partner work. I saw Jennifer and Niveah make their reading match their pictures when at first it didn't. And I saw Sammy and Bryan make their characters talk."

I then hung a premade mini-chart of these three steps on my easel as a more visual reminder. I was already imagining that my kids would need more support during their extended partner time today than I could possibly offer, and I hoped our new "Powerful Partners Work as a Team!" chart would provide some of that support.

As I named the three steps for doing this work, I made sure to touch each one. "When you try to make your reading better and better, first you want to reread the chart to remember what makes it better. Then, see-saw read and listen closely. And, finally, check your reading every few pages."

Powerful Partners Work as a Team!

- Reread the chart. (We Are Storybook Readers!)
- Decide how to read. (see-saw)
- Stop and check your reading.

"Today, readers, we won't have private reading time. Instead, I want you to do this partner work with as many old favorite storybooks as you can today. So, off you go to read with the person next to you at your table and from your table tubs. Try to wow your partner when they are the listener." I flipped our sign to Partner Reading, and the kids hurried off.

Challenging Partners to Stop and Check Their Reading

BECAUSE THE ENTIRE READING TIME WILL BE PARTNER READING, it will be important to keep your kids moving from book to book. Your hope is that each partnership will read and then reread three to five old favorite storybooks during this time. (Remember that many children have personalized old favorites from home too. Make sure they use them with their partners.) Voiceovers can help you keep your partnerships moving from book to book so that you have more time to coach into their partner work. Every five minutes or so, you might call out to the room something like "How many people have finished working with one book and are now working on book number two?" or "How many people are reading a book again?"

You will mostly want to spend time today supporting the stopping and checking work partnerships are doing as they read. Stopping and checking your reading is perhaps the most important behavior you can get readers, especially beginning readers, to do. You can anticipate that the vast majority of your kids will not stop every page or two to think about their reading or the book. Be ready to be the stopper and the prompter of stopping, and then be ready to repeat that move again and again as you move from partnership to partnership. Remember that in the end, it does not really matter how much better their reading becomes after stopping; what really matters now is that kindergarten readers get in the habit of stopping and thinking as they read.

The work during this session also gives you a chance to think about what partnerships will look like going forward in your class. At some point very soon, you will want to assign kids to more permanent partnerships. Today, watch for how kids encourage each other to do better work. You will also want to notice how much fun they have together and how equally they share the work. Jot notes about these behaviors, and plan to use them soon to create productive, longer-term partnerships.

MID-WORKSHOP TEACHING
Showing How Partners Reread to Sound More Like the Book

"Readers, I want to interrupt for a minute. Can I give you a tip? Once you stop and check your reading, then you need to make your reading better. Rereading is definitely a way you can do that. After you check your reading, you will probably want to reread some of the pages that you realized might be better.

"When I was sitting with Balla and Marcella, they reread one page in *The Carrot Seed*. They made the last page sound much more like the book because they tried it again and used exact words. And because they had done that together, they high-fived each other!" I high-fived Marcella and Bala.

"I wonder if there will be more retries and better reading and more high fives out there in the next few minutes. Raise your hand if you think that could be you."

Transitioning to Learn-about-the-World Reading

Invite children to read their learn-about-the-world books, using a familiar chart to check their reading.

"Readers, as you choose learn-about-the-world books from the table tubs today, I was thinking that we could use our 'Readers LEARN from Books, Too!' chart from a few weeks ago to help us do the same reading and checking and making-better work in our learn-about-the-world books."

I pointed to our chart from the first bend of the unit, and I quickly read it so my class could remember what was on it.

> **ANCHOR CHART**
>
> Readers LEARN from Books, Too!
>
> - We learn from pictures.
> - We learn from words.
> - We sound like a teacher.

"With your learn-about-the-world books, you can use the chart to read these books better too. Don't forget how much rereading helps." I then returned to our "Readers Read with a Partner" chart from earlier in the session. I reminded my readers of the steps to take with their learn-about-the-world books. I sent them off to work together some more.

At the end of today's reading workshop, you will want to think about your word study. By this point in the first unit, you will probably have done name study on almost all of your students. You will probably have introduced all of the letters/sounds in the alphabet too. Don't worry if your kids have not mastered all of the letter/ sounds. You can keep teaching into this knowl- edge during the next unit. However, remember that you may also have some kindergarten chil- dren who already know some letter/sounds, and you will want to be doing teaching that keeps pace with them too.

A Celebration of Old Favorite Storybook Reading (and Learn-about-the-World Reading, Too)

MINILESSON

In the connection, you might start your minilesson while the kids are still at their tables. You will want them to pick a favorite book for today's celebration. You might say something like "Readers, we are going to have a special celebration today of all the work we did to become readers! As part of that celebration, I want you to choose a book that you love *and* read really well. Right now, look through the tub at your table for that book. Remember, we practiced two kinds of reading during this unit. We read learn-about-the-world books, and we read old favorite storybooks. You can pick either kind of book. But I just want you to pick one." Give students a minute or two to choose, and then have them bring their choice to the carpet.

For the teaching point, you might say something like "Today I want to teach you that when people work hard at something and they succeed, they celebrate. And sometimes they celebrate by throwing a parade."

During your teaching, you will want to remind the kids of the work they did in both kinds of books by putting up your anchor charts and recruiting them to read the charts with you, shared reading style.

For the active engagement, encourage students to practice their book all the way through, using the chart that matches to check their reading. You might say, "Think about the chart that matches your book. If you have an old favorite storybook, use our 'We Are Storybook Readers!' chart, and if you are holding a learn-about-the-world book, use our 'Readers LEARN from Books, Too!' chart. Point to the chart you'll use. Ready, now use our charts to do your very best reading!"

In your link, you will want to encourage readers to practice the book they chose multiple times. Make sure that your readers know how long they have to practice their books. Perhaps you will give your kids ten minutes to read and reread their books before you switch them to partner reading time.

CONFERRING AND SMALL-GROUP WORK

During your conferences and small-group work, spend time highlighting the tremendous growth your young readers have made. "A few weeks ago, you were pointing at the picture and saying words. You worked so hard to make your reading stronger, and now, you sound like the book! Wow! You are really growing." Try to get to as many readers as possible, sharing with them personal stories about how they have grown. See yourself as the class historian when you do their conferring work. Your job is too tell the story of how your students hve grown in this unit. And going forward, you will continue to chronicle their amazing learning journey.

Mid-Workshop Teaching

For your mid-workshop teaching point, be responsive to the needs of your students. This is your final opportunity within this unit to support the work your students are doing. Perhaps your students will be reading words without connecting across pages, and you'll remind them to use connecting words to join the pages in their books.

Transition to Partner Time

For partner reading, partners could each take a turn reading their book to one another. You might give another ten minutes to this work, and then you will want to begin your parade!

CELEBRATION

You might begin by saying, "In our parade today, just like the parades that teams throw when they win championships, we will want to show off our trophy to the world. *Our* trophies are books. I thought that to make our books look a little extra special, we might put these stick-on bows on the covers." Let your kids do the bow-sticking.

Then, have everyone gather up their books and get in line. You might say, "Readers, let's go celebrate our hard work!" You will probably want to give some warning to the rest of the school. (Parades, after all, can be quite disruptive.) You will want to have already decided your parade route, and you might even have arranged for "crowds" to line it. If you really want to go over the top, you might add some parade music via a portable wireless speaker, and some of the crowd members could hold celebratory signs with sayings like "We love kindergarten readers" or "The Carrot Seed Rocks."

After your kids have walked the parade route holding up their books and receiving the adoration of the crowd, you will want to end up somewhere for a little celebratory reading. If you choose this option, be sure to have the teacher prepare her class for the fact that your kindergarten students will not yet be reading conventionally. Visiting another class is a great option, perhaps a class of older kids. Or you might bring students to a special location in the school, such as the school library, where listeners have convened to hear a final reading by each child.

Once everyone has read and talked a little about their books with a partner, you will want to close your celebration in some way.

SHARE

Today's share session might involve the kids receiving a symbolic "key to the city" like athletes often do at the end of a championship parade. You might call it the "key to the reading world at your school," and you could make a cardboard key to give to each child. You might make this work feel even more special by inviting the principal or librarian to come and present students with their keys. Alternatively, you might celebrate by giving students copies of books. You would have to figure out how to make this happen, per-haps by using book club points to order books for students. Call every child up and cheer for them and the tremendous growth they have made as readers.

After your whole class has been called and clapped for, you might have them join you in reading the last line of *The Three Billy Goats Gruff* as the final word on the celebration and this unit.

The last line is "So Snip! Snap! Snout! This tale's told out!" If you do decide to end like this, have this line visible for the whole class on chart paper. Then you might say, "This is the end of our celebration. This is the end of our unit. You have become readers. You *are* readers."

After making some eye contact with everyone, say, "I thought we might signal the end of our work the way our billy goats book does." Have them then read that line one time, two times, three times, until everyone has joined in and you are all reading loud.

And that's it. You've successfully launched a lifelong reading journey for your kindergarten students.

Snip! Snap! Snout! This *unit's* told out!

Read-Aloud

Getting Ready: BOOK SELECTION

Book selection will be hugely important. We selected *The Carrot Seed*, by Ruth Krauss, because it is a tightly structured story and yet brief and accessible enough that once your children have heard it often, some will be able to approximate reading the actual words.

Be sure to choose a book that, first of all, your students enjoy. Because they will hear this book again and again, it is important that they really like it. The book should also have a strong plot with a pretty traditional narrative structure to develop your kids' sense of how stories go. In other words, the story should have clear characters who go through a series of events and face troubles that, in the end, are resolved somehow.

A powerful emergent storybook also has rich language that is more academic. In other words, you need to choose a book that talks more like books do and less like we all do in social situations. These books are usually higher-level books, too. They tend to have more multisyllabic words and more sentences per page. Before finalizing your selection of books, make sure you have multiple copies so that you'll be able to put copies into the hands of at least half your kids the following week. Your children will reread this book many, many times, so providing them copies is essential and worth the trouble. Ideally, you'll also want to select books available in Big Book format or ones that you can enlarge using a document camera or Smart Board. For the first few days, however, don't use an enlarged copy; reading aloud the book first will keep the focus on the language and content of the story, rather than the actual print.

The Carrot Seed, by Ruth Krauss. Illustrated by Crockett Johnson.

Goals/Rationale/Prelude

Across the read-aloud time during this first unit, your aim will be to support students' growing understanding of story structure and concepts about print while developing language and building vocabulary. You'll support much of this work by repeatedly reading emergent storybooks. This instruction, based on the research of Elizabeth Sulzby, is described in Chapter 4 of *A Guide to the Reading Workshop: Primary Grades*. Each day, you'll probably do one read-aloud before workshop and a second read-aloud after workshop.

Emergent storybooks also make great additions to choice time in your kindergarten class. Choice time may involve thirty to forty-five minutes set aside at the end of each day. This is time for your kids to dictate how and what they will learn. In many kindergarten classrooms, there are centers that kids choose and then remain in for the whole period. These centers may include painting, Legos, puzzles, and blocks. Kids may choose action figures and dramatic play in the "kitchen." They might also play dress up.

Many kindergarten teachers also have a writing center decked out with cool paper choices and writing implements and awesome scissors, so that kids can do the writing projects they cannot get to in writing workshop. During this unit, children can also have an old favorite storybook center. The books can be in a basket in the center, and kids can be encouraged to bring these books to life. Puppets or masks and scenery can be made and then books can be acted out. Sometimes children even make mash-ups of their books, where several stories combine to make a new one!

Throughout these sessions, your goal will be to invite students to participate with you in a collaborative reading. When you read *The Carrot Seed* as you would read a bedtime story, encouraging children to participate, your goal is for children to chime in often. They'll suggest what might come next, they'll fill in the upcoming events and reactions to events, drawing mostly on their memory of the story and also on the pictures. You'll still only be reading the small copy of the text, and there will be no expectation that children rely on the print.

After you reread *The Carrot Seed* (or the alternative book you select) repeatedly throughout this week, your hope is that your kids will be able to reconstruct the storyline as they make their way through the book on their own (assuming most won't actually be able to read the words). At least some of your children will attend to the print when they "read" this book (and soon, other very lean, accessible stories.) Even children with little prior experience with written language should be able, within a week, to turn the pages of *The Carrot Seed* and progress through it from front to back, pretending to read it as best they can.

Highlight, through your actions, the fact that readers progress from the front cover, through the pages of a story, to the back. Show children that when readers turn to a new page, they look at the picture, notice what's going on, and think,

"How does this fit into the story I remember?" Recruit kids to help you study the picture, recall the story, and access their memory of this page.

Lastly, on Day Five, you will not want to forget to talk about the book. These discussions can take many different formats.

SESSIONS 1 AND 2

BEFORE YOU READ

Introduce the book, providing a gist of the story.

"This is a story called *The Carrot Seed*. It's written by Ruth Krauss and the pictures are by Crockett Johnson. In this story a little boy plants a carrot seed and everyone in his family tells him it won't grow!"

Take a book walk, scanning over a few important pages, recruiting the kids to say aloud what they see in ways that construct the gist of the story.

"Let's take a peek at some of the pages."

"What's the little boy doing? What's in his hand?" "Look what's happening here!" After suggestions from kids, "You think so? Could be."

Choose a couple pages in a row and then skip one. Don't read every single page.

Pages 6–7: Point to the details in the illustrations to channel readers to look closely, and prompt them to say what's on the page.

"There's the little boy. What did he do first? That's right, he planted a carrot seed. What else do you see? Yes, there's a shovel. Oh, that must be the seed packet he opened to get the carrot seed."

Pages 4–9: Recruit kids to figure out who the new characters might be and what they might be saying and doing.

Drawing on your knowledge of the text, tell the children what the characters are saying and doing, re-creating the storyline with them. Then prompt a prediction, and read on.

A little boy planted
a carrot seed.

"Who might this be? Yes, this must be his mother. I wonder what she said. Yes, maybe. Maybe she's telling the little boy the carrot seed won't grow." Turn the page. "Do you think this is the father? I bet he tells the little boy it won't grow, too." Turn the page. "His big brother is pointing at the ground. I don't think he thinks the seed will grow either! Oh my goodness!

"What do you think will happen next? Will the carrot seed come up? Thumbs up if you think his carrot will grow! Thumbs down if you think it won't come up! Let's read and find out what happens."

AS YOU READ *Read text*

Read the text straight through with expression, incorporating simple gestures and engaging the students to chime in and gesture along with you during this first read.

As you open the book and begin to read the words, remember that the pictures tell children which part of the story should be fastened onto which page. That is, you could say that the pictures anchor the story onto specific pages. Therefore, when you approach a new page, use your finger and perhaps your words to focus children's attention on the part of the picture that signals the relevant part of the story.

On page 2 you can look at the picture and pretend you are planting a seed. When you reach the page where the boy is kneeling beside his carrot to weed it, you need this picture to signal to children that this is a picture of the boy weeding his carrot. So as you look at that picture, name it in a way that will do the job of anchoring the text to the page. Say, "Oh look, he is weeding." That is, talk about the pictures in ways that match the content and language of the story.

Tiny pauses as you read are silent invitations for your students to join in. Turn to a new page, look at it yourself, and then look at your class, expectantly. Leave invitations for them to call out, to chime in, and use your hands to welcome their contributions. You needn't discuss what children say. Welcome their ideas, then read the page, and perhaps the next page, before again inviting input. After you have read about what the mother and father said, you may read, "And his big brother said . . ." Most likely your class will chime into the pattern of the text and say, "It won't come up."

Think ahead of time about what you will want your children to do when they read on their own. Then—once you have figured that out—do whatever that is yourself, over and over again, as you read. If you want your children to study the picture before attempting to read the words, then do that. Turn the page and immediately, use your finger to show that you are taking in parts of the picture. Do that exact same thing again and again, and in time, signal for kids to join you in doing it.

If you want students to read with more drama in their voices, do that as well! Dramatize the voices of the characters to help signal students to new characters talking on the page. You can use your voice, facial expressions, and gestures to help convey the feelings and tone of the characters.

SESSION 1: AS YOU READ

p. 2: Read the text straight through with expression, incorporating simple gestures and inviting students to gesture along with you.

AFTER YOU READ—WHOLE-CLASS BOOK TALK

Quickly retell the key details as a class to support comprehension of the text.

"Let's turn back to the beginning and think about all the parts of this story to retell what happened in *The Carrot Seed*. What happened first? Yes, the little boy planted a carrot seed in the ground. And then . . ." Leave spaces for children to chime in to fill in the details as you turn back through the pages of the text. "His mother said, 'It won't come up!' You're right! His whole family didn't think the carrot seed would grow. What happened next? Turn and retell with your partner."

Listen in to students retelling before reconvening to retell key details.

"I heard you say that the little boy pulled out the weeds and gave it water, and he waited and waited and waited. And finally, at the end, a carrot came up! How do you think the little boy felt at the end of the story? Turn and tell your partner and use the word *because* to say why."

"Let's share some of what you heard. When you hear something you agree with and you think, 'Yeah, me too! I think the same thing,' will you put your thumb up on your knee?"

"These are all really good ideas. I agree that the boy must've felt so happy that his carrot seed grew into an enormous carrot! Maybe he even feels proud. That was hard work! He was so patient! What a great story! Let's read it again tomorrow! Maybe even more voices will help me read next time."

SESSIONS 3 AND 4

Turn & Tell your partner what happened in the book

BEFORE YOU READ

"We are going to read *The Carrot Seed* again! Who remembers how the story goes? Can you quickly remind your friend next to you what happens in the book? Turn and tell!"

Invite students to chime in as the text becomes increasingly more familiar.

You might say, "This time, let's hear even more voices read along with me as we get to parts you know! Let's all read *The Carrot Seed* together with our best storyteller voices, and use your hands to act out parts. Let's bring this story to life!"

AS YOU READ

You'll want to engage the class in reading along with you, acting out with simple gestures, and reciting the lines with more expression now that the text is becoming more familiar. Look to see that more students are participating. To recruit for more participation and voices to chime in, you may say to your students, "Act this part out with me! Use your hands!" or "Let's reread that part together! Let's make our voices sound like the father."

You may also decide to do some very lean think-alouds that help show the decisions that you are making. For example, you might say, "How would he sound here? Let's read this part again and make him sound doubtful!" or you might say, "Show me with your face and body how the little boy is feeling here. Let's reread this page showing how he feels on our faces."

Because you want children to pay attention to language in their emergent storybooks, you will want to do so during your read-aloud. Lines that repeat make for good places to emphasize exactly how the book "talks." You will want to encourage your readers to try to talk exactly like the book does in more and more places as they come to know the book better and better.

SESSION 2: AS YOU READ

pp. 10–11: Prompt students to act out what the character is doing.

"You guys pretend to be the character and act like him/her as you listen to the words I am reading."

AFTER YOU READ—BRIEF TEACHER SUMMARY

Some days you will not have an opportunity to bring everyone together for a whole-class book talk. You may decide to comment, summarize, or leave your students with some final thoughts to be thinking about during the day. You may say, "Well, that little boy sure was worried, but he kept trying and trying! He didn't give up either, did he? I wonder why. Why didn't he give up? I hope we can be just like that little boy in this class! We can work hard and try hard and play hard—and just not give up! A new motto for our class!"

SESSION 5

BEFORE YOU READ

Channel students to do some new thinking work across this final reading of the book.

"This time as we read *The Carrot Seed*, let's really think about this little boy and how he feels across the story and what ideas we have about him. When you're having an idea about the little boy, put a thumb on your knee. Let's read together! Maybe you can even do it without my voice in some parts!"

AS YOU READ

By now, the story will be very familiar to children, and you'll want to use this final reading as an opportunity to deepen comprehension, responding, and moving beyond the text. You'll prompt students to think and turn and talk to share their ideas. You might allow your voice to fall out in places, allowing students' voices to grow stronger. (See Day Five Post-it prompts pack for transferable notes to place across your copy of the text.)

A little boy planted a carrot seed.

His mother said, "I'm afraid it won't come up."

His mother said, "I'm afraid it won't come up."

"I'm looking at the boy's face and I think he must be thinking something in his head. Maybe he is thinking, 'Oh no! Really? I'm not worried at all. I know it will grow up!' I don't think he is bothered. I think he is confident. Thumbs up if you think, 'Me too!' or thumbs sideways if you think something different. Interesting. Let's keep reading. Wait, what's going to happen next?" Say this almost like a rhetorical question, and don't wait for responses. Just continue reading.

His father said, "I'm afraid it won't come up."

"What's going to happen next? Turn and tell your partner."

"You think it's his big brother? Thumbs up, you agree. Thumbs sideways, you think something different."

And his big brother said, "I'm afraid it won't come up."

"You were right! It's his big brother. Let's keep reading."

Every day the little boy pulled up the weeds around the seed and sprinkled the ground with water.

"How can we describe who this little boy is? How does he act and behave? Let's try to use lots of words to talk about him. I think he is a smart boy because he knows how to take care of plants. I think he works super hard. What else can we say about him? Turn and talk to your partners. 'I think the little boy is . . . He is the kind of person who . . . He is acting . . .'"

"Give me a thumbs up if you agree with your friends. I heard people say things like, 'He is strong because he is pulling up weeds,' and 'He hopes a carrot will grow,' and 'He is the kind of boy who won't give up.' I also agree with all of these things! I know there are more things that you said, but we need to finish the book now. Let's read to the end and think about who this boy is and how he feels at the end."

But nothing came up.

And nothing came up.

"So frustrating! But he doesn't look frustrated does he? He looks . . ." Inviting a few to answer. "Yes, patient, hopeful, curious, and calm. Let's keep reading."

Everyone kept saying it wouldn't come up.

But he still pulled up the weeds around it everyday and sprinkled the ground with water.

"Turn and talk. Say everything you know about the boy! 'I think he feels . . . He's the kind of character who . . . I think he is . . .'"

"I heard, 'Hard working, nice because he is taking care of the plants, good, smart, patient.' Me too! You, too! Great, let's finish the book."

And then, one day,

a carrot came up

just as the little boy had known it would.

"Okay, what happened here? What does that mean, 'just as the little boy had known it would'? Let me reread that last line. I think it means just *like* the little boy had known it would. Just *as* and just *like* mean the same thing, I think. Turn and talk about the ending with your partners. Why does the book end with that line? Why doesn't it just say, 'And then one day a carrot came up'?"

AFTER YOU READ—PERFORM THE BOOK!

Assign groups of students to act out the roles in *The Carrot Seed*, with several children playing the role of the little boy. Another group can act as the mother, and so forth. Turn the pages of the book to reenact the scenes. Coach readers with prompts, such as "Match your voice." "Show the feeling." "What did that part look like?" "Act it out!"

Shared Reading

Text Selection

> *Mrs. Wishy-Washy*, by Joy Cowley. Illustrations by Elizabeth Fuller.

> A familiar nursery rhyme of your choice, for example, "Jack and Jill"

We chose *Mrs. Wishy-Washy*, by Joy Cowley, because it provides an engaging storyline with repetition that young readers can hold onto. At this time in the year you'll want to choose texts that are fun to read or may present rhyme and pattern to support children in phonological awareness and help them hold onto the text. Overall, these books should be great fun and accessible, because this is a time to welcome children into the world of print. Shared reading was initially designed to mimic a child sitting on the lap of an adult, interacting with text together. These are the joyful moments that inspire children's love of reading. Brenda Parkes has written many texts that are ideal for shared reading, in addition to a wonderful, easy-to-read professional book on shared reading, *Read It Again: Revisiting Shared Reading* (Stenhouse, 2000).

Goals/Rationale/Prelude

- What follows is a five-day plan for shared reading. This plan is particularly helpful if your goal is to have children come to know a book very well. It also mimics the rereading work that kids are expected to do in a reading workshop. As you take children through five days of work in the same book, you are showing them how to return to a text again and again to get more and more out of it. You are showing them how fun it is to come to know a book by heart.

- However, we also want to acknowledge that there are other ways to plan for shared reading. For instance, you may decide to do a *different* book each day of the week. This kind of shared reading work is particularly important if you want to show your kids how the reading process works in many different kinds of books. You may choose this plan when you want to get your readers involved in using a repertoire of strategies to make meaning from text. Also, if you want to expose your kids to a variety of text types, a book a day can be more powerful than a book a week.

- In the end, you will want to use the needs of your class to make decisions about which type of shared reading plan to use. If you choose the different book a day plan, you will need to do the work of all *five* of our days in this plan *in one day* for each book. In other words, you will want to integrate into one reading, as opposed to separate across several readings, the reading work that kids need to learn to do to make big meaning from their books.

DAY ONE: Falling in Love with the Book

Start by introducing the book and predict, along with the children, what the book might be about, using the title and the cover illustration. Be careful not to overdo this part; you want to spend most of your time reading! Then, you'll read the book, inviting children to chime in even on this first read. You'll be amazed how many leap right in! As you read, you'll want to take some time to look closely at the pictures with children. (Remember, you'll have all week for this work, so make careful choices about where to pause and where to keep reading.) To teach early concepts about print, emphasize book handling skills, along with crisp pointing, to reinforce directionality and one-to-one match. At times you might make purposeful mistakes like reading backward or setting the book upside down on the easel, leaving space for the kids to correct you. After all, students love catching teachers' mistakes! After reading, you'll want to support important comprehension skills, such as retelling key details.

DAY ONE FOCUS

✔ Rally your emergent readers to say, "Of course I can read!"

✔ Build classroom community around reading.

✔ Develop early concepts about print, language structure, phonological awareness (rhyming and wordplay), and of course, comprehension.

WARM UP: A Familiar Text

Quickly reread a familiar text (a poem, song, chant, chart, or the word wall) to build confidence, excitement, and fluency.

To warm your class up for reading, read a familiar song or nursery rhyme such as "Jack and Jill." You'll read the text and try to get their voices to chime in. You might say, "Readers, to warm up today, let's read 'Jack and Jill.' I'll point to the words as we all share the reading. Will you join in with me?"

You'll want to do some rereading to get the children to participate, saying things like "Let's reread this part about Jack falling down and see if we can get more voices to read together!" As more readers chime in, point to them, nodding and celebrating. "Yes! I hear you reading now, too!"

BOOK INTRODUCTION AND FIRST READING: *Mrs. Wishy-Washy*, by Joy Cowley

Give a book introduction to provide a gist of the story and entice readers.

Recruit the class to join in a shared reading of a book that will thread its way across the week and eventually the year: *Mrs. Wishy-Washy*. This will be one of the class's favorite books, so create enthusiasm for the text right away. As you place an enlarged copy of the book on the easel, you might say, "This is one of my all-time favorite books. It tells the story of a lady named Mrs. Wishy-Washy who lives on a farm with lots of animals. But the big problem in this story is that those animals are covered in mud. They're *so* dirty! What do you think will happen?"

You may decide to preview the text.

Talk about the cover and do a picture walk, recruiting the class to join you in a sneak peek of the first few pages. Don't tarry long, however, turning this into instructional time, because the main goal is to *read*. Read, aiming above all for the class to have a blast with the book.

Read the book from cover to cover, with a fluent and expressive voice. Invite children to chime in right from the start.

Avoid reading in a staggered way, slowing down to match the voices of your readers. Instead, model how the book ought to sound. This will silently urge kids to catch up to you. You'll find that the group develops momentum as you read along, and before you know it, your meeting area will be filled with smiling, engaged readers.

You'll want to find at least one place to stop and turn and talk about the story.

You might say, "I wonder what is going to happen next?" or "Wait, how would Mrs. Wishy-Washy *really* say that?" You will also invite kids to use their bodies to act out parts of the story: "Can we read that again, the *wishy-washy, wishy-washy* part? This time, let's get our hands ready so we can pretend we are scrubbing the animals, too!"

Consider opportunities to build vocabulary.

As you read, you may decide to highlight the meaning of *paddled*. Model how you use context clues, details in the illustration, and in some cases, acting out gestures to understand the meaning of new words. You may say, "Hmm, . . . *paddled*. Well it says, 'and she paddled in it,' so I think it's something the duck is *doing*, in the mud. I see here in the picture the duck is moving her feet back and forth through the mud. Maybe it looks like this." Act it out, paddling your hands back and forth. "Okay, ducks, everybody paddle!" Once everyone has paddled, you might say, "Nice paddling, duckies. You know what? Your duck hands looked a little like a paddle for a boat. Let's pretend we need to move a boat. Let's use our paddle to paddle." As we pretended to move our boats, we said, "Paddle, paddle, paddle."

REREADING WITH A FOCUS

Reread all (or part) of *Mrs. Wishy Washy*, emphasizing different things readers do each time.

Once you have read through the entire text, reread the story at least once or twice, to offer additional practice with the skills you're supporting kindergartners to use independently. On your first focused rereading, for example, you may highlight early concepts of print. Weave this work into reading. "Okay, ready to reread the story?" you can say, turning the book upside down and backward. "Does it go like that? No! Silly me! Who can come up and fix this book so we can

7

Vocabulary work is most powerful when it is done both in the context of the book and elsewhere. New words are more likely to become a permanent fixture in kids' language when they use those words immediately and frequently. That's why I had the kids chanting, with me.

reread it together?" You may voice over things like "Wait, let's look at the front cover. Here's the picture. Now, where is the title? Oh! Here it is. Read it with me." Or "Look at the title page. What might this mean? Think about the cover and the title to help you." Then as you turn the pages of the book, you can highlight how you move through the book page by page, reading left to right. You can recruit kids to point to the first word on each page to support directionality. You might stop and ask kids to count the words on a particular page, as you point word by word with a pointer.

AFTER READING

Conduct a wrap-up activity at the end of the book such as a whole-class shared retelling of the parts of the book.

Say to your students, "Whoa! That was really fun to read! I wonder how many of you remember *all* the things that happened in the story? Let's see if we can work together to remember how the story went. Let's see if we can remember all the events, the things that happened. I am going to keep track of them on my fingers! I'll start at the beginning. I remember that the animals were jumping in the mud. They were getting really dirty. Who can add on? What happened next? Claudette, go!"

After your students retell what happened in the text, you may even prompt them to turn and talk quickly and retell once again, this time in pairs, to remember all the parts in *Mrs. Wishy-Washy*. Then say, "Books are so much fun to read and reread and reread again! They are like the games you play outside! We will get to read this book *many* times! I bet we'll make our reading voices better and better each time. I wonder what we will notice and remember in the book tomorrow!"

DAY TWO: Looking Closely at Pictures

On this day, you'll reread the book with a focus on looking closely at the pictures to develop ideas about the text and predict. Spend ample time exploring the pictures, prompting students to draw as much meaning from them as they can.

WARM UP: A Familiar Text

Quickly reread a familiar text (i.e., a poem, song, chant, chart, the word wall) to build confidence and excitement and get voices ready.

You may return to "Jack and Jill." If so, invite a student to come up and use the pointer for the warm up, reinforcing one-to-one correspondence, as the students read.

DAY TWO FOCUS

- ✔ Rally emergent readers to say, "Of course I can read!"
- ✔ Build classroom community around reading.
- ✔ Develop early concepts about print, language structure, phonological awareness (rhyming and wordplay), and of course, comprehension.
- ✔ Study pictures to notice more details.

SECOND READING: *Mrs. Wishy-Washy*

As you read today, you'll place an emphasis on studying the pictures. You might start by saying, "Readers, we can learn so much about the story by looking closely at the pictures. Today we'll be just like detectives searching the pictures to learn even more about the story." You might pause at various pages, encouraging students to look again, pushing themselves to notice even more about each page, uncovering new details. For example, on page 14, you might spend a minute studying the illustration. Kids might notice how Mrs. Wishy-Washy is walking back to her farmhouse, which is behind a fence far from the animals. They might also notice how the animals are watching her walk away. They might consider what the animals are thinking as Mrs. Wishy-Washy walks away. They might notice that the animals are much cleaner now and still dripping wet.

Teach readers to use characters' facial expressions to consider how they feel.

For example, on page 5, you may want to look at the pig, paying extra attention to his expression as he rolls in the mud. "Let's look closely at this pig. How do you think he might feel right now?" Prompt students to show the feeling with their own facial expressions or body language as you reread to match your reading voice.

Cover a few of the words, encouraging children to use the picture and the pattern to read.

Of course, since most children are not yet reading conventionally, you may simply pause mid-sentence, rather than physically mask words. Prompt kids to figure it out. "What might this word be?" or "How do you think this sentence goes?" Encourage students to rely on meaning by prompting, "Let's use the picture to help us with the words." Encourage students to rely on structure/syntax, by prompting, "Let's think about the pattern. How does this book talk?" For example, on page 6, you might cover the word *duck* to prompt students to use the picture as a source of information. On another page, you might cover the word *lovely* to prompt students to hold onto the pattern to read.

AFTER READING

Have students turn and talk to their partners to discuss the text.

You might prompt readers to retell again, thinking about *all* the parts of the story. You might ask students to think about the new things they noticed in the pictures and then add those new things into their retelling. You might even pose some reflection questions such as "How did the pictures help us understand the story better?" or "How did the pictures help us read the words?"

On this day, you'll focus on word play activities relevant to the work students need at these levels, primarily phonological awareness. This day might look more like inquiry, studying particular word study concepts and hunting for words or features. Word study includes several important concepts: concepts about print (at the book and the word level), phonological awareness, phonics, and high-frequency word recognition. The power of shared reading is that it gives all kids access to print at their level of literacy understanding. So while some kids will be developing the concept of one-to-one match, others may be recognizing high-frequency words. At this point in the year, you might choose to have your kindergartners play with rhyming words, hunt for letters, or clap syllables.

DAY THREE FOCUS

✔ Develop phonological awareness.

✔ Highlight patterns.

✔ Play with rhyme.

WARM UP: A Familiar Text

Quickly reread a familiar text (i.e., a poem, song, chant, chart, the word wall) to build confidence and excitement and get voices ready.

Since you'll focus today's work around words, you may want to choose a rhyming text, such as "Little Miss Muffet" or "One, Two, Buckle My Shoe." You might have students name each rhyming word of the text, coming up to highlight the word. Then, reading the poem once again, place even more emphasis on the rhyming words.

THIRD READING: *Mrs. Wishy-Washy*

Today you will focus on word study. You'll want to tailor this work to the needs of your students.

Consider the concepts your students most need based on recent assessments and observations. For example, you might find that your students need continued practice solidifying early concepts about print, such as book handling, directionality, or one-to-one correspondence. Students might also need support with phonological awareness—listening for rhyme, letter sound, or syllables. Or, you might choose to focus on letter and word identification to reinforce phonics and/or high-frequency words. Choose one or two areas your students most need, and practice those skills in multiple places in the text. To do this, you might begin by first reading the whole book and then going back to several pages to study the letters and words, or by reading a page or two and then stopping to practice these skills. Below, we've outlined a few possible activities you might choose to engage in across this third reading.

Continue to support students' growing understanding of print concepts.

For example, you might pause at the start of a new page and think aloud, "Hmm, . . . how many words are on this page? Let's count them together. Now, Brandon, come up and point under each word as we all read this page together. Make it match!"

Develop students' phonological awareness.

Choose a specific letter sound. This could be the first letter of a child's name. Ask students to clap if they hear a word that starts with that sound. You might say, "As I read this next page, listen closely for words that start with /w/ like *William*. If you hear a word that starts the same way, clap once!"

Highlight familiar word wall words as you read.

You might start by saying, "Let's look at our class word wall and remember the 'snap' words we've learned so far. Read them with me!" After reading these words in isolation, from a nearby word wall or a pocket chart, invite students to hunt for these words in the class shared text. You might say, "If you spot one of our 'snap' words in *Mrs. Wishy-Washy*, snap your fingers! Then, we can stop and put highlighting tape to make those words pop!"

AFTER READING

Play a quick rhyming game with students, choosing a few words from the book to use.

For example, "Let's see if we can make lots of rhyming words with *pig*." You might even create a signal for when you rhyme with real words, and another signal for when you rhyme with nonsense words. "Readers, when we rhyme, sometimes we think of real words and sometimes we make up silly words. When we say a real word, put your finger on your nose. When we say a silly word, put your finger on your shoulder."

Sing a rhyming song such as "Willaby Wallaby Woo" to transition students off the rug and back to their seats. Do some phonemic substitution. "Willaby Wallaby Wuke, an elephant sat on . . ." Pause and wait for Luke to stand up. Dismiss his entire table so that you don't have to sing every name off the rug. Just one child at a time will work.

DAY FOUR: Fluency

On this day, you'll focus on fluency, helping children to read accurately, at the proper rate, and with prosody. Prosody involves making sure the text sounds right. You will help your children get the right phrasing, intonation, and stress. So much of getting the sound right in a book has to do with paying attention to punctuation.

WARM UP: A Familiar Text

Quickly reread a familiar text (i.e., a poem, song, chant, chart, the word wall) to build confidence and excitement and get voices ready.

You might return, once again, to "Jack and Jill." This time, drop the volume of your voice, allowing students to lead the shared reading. You'll want to encourage students to bring this same confidence to the fourth reading of your shared

DAY FOUR FOCUS

✔ Rally emergent readers to say, "Of course I can read!"

✔ Build classroom community around reading.

✔ Develop early concepts about print, language structure, phonological awareness (rhyming and wordplay), and of course, comprehension.

✔ Study pictures to notice more details.

✔ Read with fluency.

text. You might say, "Wow! You read this with such smooth voices. You didn't even need my help! I bet you could read *Mrs. Wishy-Washy* with those same strong, smooth voices."

FOURTH READING: *Mrs. Wishy-Washy*

While reading with fluency and expression, invite children to join you in putting stress on certain words or phrases, developing prosody.

Mrs. Wishy-Washy offers a variety of opportunities to practice fluency. On page 9, the word *look* is written in a way that cues readers to emphasize the word when reading aloud. You can practice this same work on the last page, with the phrase, "Oh, lovely mud."

Act out parts of the book.

Prompt children to make their voices sound like those of the characters. You might assign four small groups, dividing the meeting area into quadrants—one each for the cow, the pig, the duck, and Mrs. Wishy-Washy. Gesture toward each group to perform (and read) their parts.

Pay attention to punctuation cues.

Help students think about how to make their reading voices match. For example, on page 9, you might say, "Wait! Let's think about the kind of punctuation mark at the end of this sentence. What do you see here? Yes, that's an exclamation mark. We'll have to make our voices a little bit louder when we read this page. Let's reread this sentence one more time."

AFTER READING

Engage the class in a discussion about the characters.

You might prompt students to think about how the animals felt when they were playing in the mud and how those feelings changed across the different parts of the story. Then, prompt students to think about Mrs. Wishy-Washy's feelings across the story.

Stir some debate!

Ask, "Should the animals have jumped back in the mud after Mrs. Wishy-Washy scrubbed them to make them clean?" Encourage students to share their opinions and use the pictures in the book to explain their thinking.

"Just **look** at you!" she screamed.

9

On this day, you'll put it all together, encouraging children to read as independently as they can. You'll also take the time to extend the text, perhaps through interactive writing, drama, or talking about the book. Small copies of the book can then be made available for children to read on their own, as well as any interactive writing you add or create.

WARM UP: A Familiar Text

Quickly reread a familiar text (i.e., a poem, song, chant, chart, the word wall) to build confidence and excitement and fluency.

If you are using "Jack and Jill," you might substitute the names of your children into the rhyme. You might have all of your kids' names written on cards that will mask *Jack* and *Jill*. Your kids might read, "Dylan and Ruby went up the hill to catch a pail of water. Dylan fell down and broke his crown, and Ruby came tumbling after." Have your kids tell you which name card to move to which spot to say the whole rhyme. "Move the one with the *r* to the last line." What nice literacy work! Your kids will love it because they are starring in the famous rhyme!

FIFTH READING: *Mrs. Wishy-Washy*

Allow students' reading voices to outshine your own, perhaps letting your voice drop entirely.

Remind readers to use strategies you've been building across the week. You might invite specific students to turn the pages or point crisply under words as the class reads along. Prompt students to problem solve if they get stuck. You might coach readers along, by saying, "Use the picture to remember how this part goes. What might the words say here?" "Remember the pattern." "Let's reread that and match our voices!"

AFTER READING

Act out the story to deepen students' comprehension of texts and support language development.

During choice time you could provide materials for students to make simple props or puppets. They could, then, use these to act out the story as they turn the pages of the book.

Engage the class in some writing connected to the text.

You might also do interactive writing with the shared text by labeling details in the pictures or adding speech bubbles across different pages. Similarly, you might add a page or change the ending. Separately, you may choose to do some shared writing with your students to support language and writing development, composing and recording a letter to the characters or the author. You might even write your own class version of the story. You'll want to place copies of any shared or interactive writing you do in students' book baggies, so they can read and approximate reading these teacher-supported materials independently during reading workshop.